D0841630

REALIZING EMPTINESS
Madhyamaka Insight Meditation

by
Gen Lamrimpa
(Lobsang Jampal Tenzin)

Translated by
B. Alan Wallace

Edited by
Ellen Posman

Snow Lion Publications
Ithaca, New York
Boulder, Colorado

Snow Lion Publications
P.O. Box 6483
Ithaca, New York 14851 USA
(607) 273-8519
www.snowlionpub.com

Second Edition USA 2002

Printed in Canada on acid-free, recycled paper.

This edition ISBN 1-55939-180-4

**The Library of Congress catalogued the previous edition of this
book as follows:**

Gen Lamrimpa, 1934-
    Realizing emptiness : the Madhyamaka cultivation of insight /
    Gen Lamrimpa (Lobsang Jampal Tenzin) ; translated by B. Alan
    Wallace ; edited by Ellen Posman.
        p.   cm.
    ISBN 1-55939-118-9
    1. Śunyata. 2. Meditation – Madhyamika (Buddhism)
    3. Vipaśyana (Buddhism) I. Wallace, B. Alan. II. Posman, Ellen.
    III. Title.
    BQ7457.G46   1999
    294.3′4435-dc21   99-31832
                                                                              CIP

Contents

Foreword

In January 1989, after leading a one-year retreat for the cultivation of meditative quiescence in the state of Washington, Gen Lamrimpa was asked by his students to give practical instructions on the cultivation of insight into the nature of emptiness. The following teachings are a record of those lectures, which were transcribed by and originally edited by Gen Lamrimpa's devoted student Pauly Fitze. At my request, the major work of editing was later done by Ellen Posman, who joined two versions of Gen Lamrimpa's narrated biography, one of them originally written down by Steven Wilhelm, into the version presented in this volume. For their invaluable contribution, I offer them my deep thanks.

After the retreat, Gen Lamrimpa also presented two lectures, one at Stanford University on the Madhyamaka view, and the other at the San Francisco Zen Center on Dzogchen. These are included here as appendices.

I was the interpreter for all the above teachings, and I have done the final editing of all these lectures, so any errors that may appear in this version are entirely my own. All of us who have worked to make these experiential teachings available to those who did not have the fortune to receive them directly from Gen Lamrimpa himself pray that this book may be of benefit to all sentient beings.

Gen Lamrimpa

A Contented Mind:
The Life of Gen Lamrimpa

The Venerable Jampal Tenzin, Gen Lamrimpa, teaches that a contented mind is within our grasp, no matter how difficult the conditions of our lives. Genla, as he is affectionately called by his students, is one of the small number of Tibetan monks who spend most of their time in solitary meditation. He makes his home in a forest hut in Sikkim, where he lives simply and engages in spiritual practices.

A visitor to the small apartment where Genla stayed during a three-month visit to Seattle was struck by the way his peaceful mind had transformed his room into a facsimile of his mountain hut. When he was not meditating or taking visitors, he would sit by the window, wrapped in a robe, studying one of the Tibetan religious texts he brought with him. "Happiness depends on the mind," Genla says, his kind, twinkling eyes looking intently at the visitor. "If we work on this, increasing the positive mind and reducing the negative mind, then we can achieve ultimate peace." But if Genla's state of mind is the embodiment of his teachings, it is not because he has led a protected or insular life—in fact, he has lived through tumult and tragedy.

Born Lobsang Jampal Tenzin in 1936 in the western Tibetan town of Shekar, in the Tingri region, Genla was groomed for the monastic life from the start. In Tibet, there are two traditions that dictate how and when one becomes a monk or a nun. The first custom is for a boy or girl to make his or her own decision after he or she has grown up. The other tradition says that when there are two boys in a family, one of them should become a monk. In accordance with this latter tradition, Genla became a novice monk at the age of seven. His father looked for a good lama at Chusang Monastery, and Lobsang Sangye became his spiritual mentor. Genla received teachings from him and received full ordination as a monk of the Gelug school of Tibetan Buddhism at the age of thirteen. He was given the name Lobsang Jampal Tenzin.

When Genla became a monk, he was very happy about the decision. Even as a little boy he remembers playing and sitting on a throne like a lama, with children sitting around him receiving teachings. At that time he was called Lama-la, and some people regarded him as *tulku*, or incarnate lama. Even adults would come to ask him questions, and he remembers saying strange things at times. Still, he does not remember now whether or not he remembered any past lives at that time.

Genla remembers his years at the monastery as a happy time of study and prayer. "Once I entered the monastery," he says, "I learned to read the scriptures, to read them very quickly in fact, and I memorized many root texts. I also learned to perform all the various rituals, make the ritual cakes for the prayers, and play the big temple horn. Since deep study was not very common in the small monasteries in Tibet back then, I learned these other things." At that time, he notes, "I didn't understand the true meaning of Dharma, particularly the purpose or reason of Dharma," and he says that he did not really comprehend the texts he was so skilled at memorizing. Like many young Tibetan males, he had been swept into his life as a monk by tradition, "like grass carried along by a river," he says.

Besides remembering this as a time of study, Genla also fondly remembers his days of mischief. At one point, a time of internal conflict at the monastery led to a lack of discipline; as a result he and some of his friends would run away from the monastery in the evenings to play dice, and would sometimes stay out all night. The next morning, exhausted, he would throw his robe over his head during prayers and doze off. When the prayers were over and everyone had left, Genla recalls with a chuckle, he would still be sitting there wrapped in his robe, fast asleep.

Later, he was put in charge of the food and the kitchen, a responsibility he performed for about two years. Then he asked his abbot to release him from that work in order to have time for study, and he also told his father that he wanted to go to Lhasa for further education. However, those first years of Genla's adulthood were dark ones, as the Chinese communists gradually tightened their control over Tibetan society. By 1959 the noose had closed, and Genla's monastery was seized by the Chinese. Genla was declared a counter-revolutionary, and the Chinese authorities ordered his capture.

Knowing His Holiness the Dalai Lama had already left Tibet, Genla resolved to flee also. Unable to even return to his room at the monastery for fear of being captured, he left all of his possessions behind and journeyed on foot with his parents over the mountains to Nepal. Genla arrived in Nepal penniless, with his shoes rotting on his feet from the monsoon rains. His mother died within the next year, and Genla found himself torn with doubts about the Dharma. "I was really struggling about whether there was any such thing as Dharma," he recalls, and says he had deep qualms about the validity of *karma:* the idea that virtuous actions bring forth happiness, and nonvirtuous actions bring unhappiness. During those many years he did a lot of contemplation and analytical meditation. After some time he came to the conclusion that the reasons supporting the relationships between good actions and happiness, and bad actions and unhappiness, proved valid, and he was able to recognize his doubts as invalid. So despite his circumstances, Genla continued his practices.

Genla stayed in Nepal for a while, first helping his family and then finding studying the Lamrim, the stages on the path to enlightenment, with the Ven. Lobsang Tsultrim. Genla went with him to Zulu Khumbu, which is very near Mt. Everest, and later he went high up into the mountains to spend his time in solitude, memorizing texts and meditating. He stayed there for seven months, sitting on a rock, not even having a cushion. At one point, his only robe, which he wore day and night, became infested with bugs. He nevertheless continued with his meditation and after several months the problem alleviated itself, and he thought that probably some purification had taken place. At that time, he claims, he did not have a very deep understanding of Dharma, but he still put in much effort.

Finally Genla was allowed to enter India, and he immediately traveled to Varanasi. There he had a private interview with Trijang Rinpoche, the Junior Tutor of His Holiness the Dalai Lama. He advised Genla to join Sera-mey College in Dalhousie. There Genla studied all the major texts, including the five principal subjects: Prajñāpāramitā (Perfection of Wisdom), Madhyamaka (Middle Way), Vinaya (Code of Ethics), Vasubandhu's *Abhidharmakośa* (*A Treasury of Knowledge*) and Dharmakīrti's *Pramāṇavārtika* (*A Commentary on Verifying Cognition*). These studies were conducted in the traditional way through logical analysis and dialectics, and Genla stayed there until 1970.

A turning point came in 1970, when Genla heard an inspiring series of lectures given by His Holiness the Dalai Lama. During the teachings His Holiness said each person should evaluate the impact of Dharma upon himself or herself, and then decide how to proceed with his or her life. His Holiness said that if one could see a good reason, then one should practice, but if one could not see the purpose, one should leave the

Dharma behind. Genla recalls that this advice helped him a lot: since he did not have any desire for wealth or possessions, it inspired him to devote his life completely to the Dharma. "After His Holiness's teachings, I felt I wanted to put my whole effort into Dharma and live a solitary life," Genla remembers. "It was very difficult to make this decision because I had no resources, and whether I could survive or not was the question."

Because Sera-mey had been supported by a health organization grant, Genla did not have any money of his own. Nevertheless, he had decided to devote his life to the Dharma, and he wanted to receive more teachings from His Holiness the Dalai Lama in Dharamsala. So in 1970, with no sponsor, he started his years of retreat, with nothing but a sack of forty pounds of flour and eighty rupees (at that time about ten dollars). Living in a hut above Dharamsala, he knew that when his food ran out he would have to go begging from door to door, so he tried to encourage himself. He kept reminding himself that the Buddha said that one who devotes his life to virtuous practices would not go hungry.

Genla feels that it was because of his good motivation that he did not have to beg once. Frequently he had to ration his food, especially when he thought he could not get a new supply for a few weeks, but he still did not have to resort to begging. As he says, "It happened consistently. Just as I was about to finish my last day's food, someone would arrive with more food." Genla realized that Buddha's speech was really true and it gave him great confidence. Moreover, Genla realized that being content and satisfied brings happiness, just as the Buddha said. For three years he did face difficulties in terms of food and lodging, and he wore the kind of rag-like robes no monks wear now, but he did not feel poor at that time. Rather, since he was satisfied, he had fewer desires, his body was more relaxed, and there was happiness in his mind. Still, Genla's spiritual practice was by no means easy—it was a matter of hard and determined effort. In particular, his second year of meditation was very difficult, with no discernible progress. At times he was tempted to leave his mountain hut, but he persevered.

During that time, Genla tried to practice patience. He encountered a government-appointed agent whose job was to look after the forest, but who despised and humiliated Genla. Trying to practice patience, Genla never responded. Looking back now, he says that though he restrained himself, his practice was still impure because it was connected with the eight mundane concerns (gain and loss, pleasure and misery, praise and blame, good and bad reputation). He realized that even after practicing this kind of patience for three years he was still thinking, "One day I will respond." Although he studied Śāntideva's text *A Guide to the Bodhisattva Way of Life*, he found that he was not able to apply the antidotes when this circumstance arose. So he did more study and more practice, and finally his anger subsided; Genla was able to generate the thought, "He is very kind to me."

At the same time, Genla realized that his conduct had become somewhat rough and did not compare well with the ways of ordinary people. He realized that when the mask of the eight mundane concerns was lifted, delusions were really directly harming him. It made him understand that whatever practice one does, if the bad is dominant that is what one will get, while if the good is dominant that is what one will get. During those years there was a great transformation in his mind and he got good results. As he says, "One can judge the results when a hardship arises that one has to face."

Hence, while Genla will only admit to a few "small" spiritual experiences as the years went by, he says the important change was in his attitude to life. "I never had qualified and authentic experiences, but I had an experience that the teachings of Dharma were valuable, and that the Dharma has a true impact on life," he says. "I was 100 percent sure that the positive mind can be increased and the negative mind reduced. I saw that this certainty exists." As Genla continued to study *tantra* and meditate on emptiness, he recalls that he had good results in his practices of love, compassion, altruism, and the spirit of awakening. "I had a good taste of these practices," he says, "but if you ask me whether I realized emptiness or the spirit of awakening, I have to say that I did not."

After many years Genla met Alan Wallace, who strongly requested that he come to the West to lead a one-year retreat on meditative quiescence. When all the conditions came together, Genla traveled to Washington State to conduct a retreat for Western practitioners at Cloud Mountain retreat center. After a year of retreat and an additional year of teaching, he returned to Dharamsala.

As a result of his experiences in the West, Genla says there is no doubt in his mind that the Dharma works here as well as in the Himalayas. "Even in a busy society, within your limitations, try to apply your own effort to practice Dharma," he says. "Buddha stated very clearly that all people have the *buddha*-nature." Still, Genla feels that Western Buddhist practitioners sometimes get confused about the various Buddhist paths, either mixing them inappropriately or falling into a form of sectarianism. Genla says to speak badly of any path is "a real mistake, a poison." Thus, one should be careful not to become sectarian, but at the same time, Genla advises that each practitioner find one particular path. "The profundity [of one school of Buddhism] for an individual is dependent on an individual's karmic imprints. Try to have faith in one school of Dharma," Genla says. "Sometimes I feel that without knowing one part of Dharma clearly, people touch every sect and teaching. They study here a little bit, there a little bit, and then there is no central practice. They are lost in-between."

Although this problem is accentuated for Westerners, who are exposed to so many types of spiritual practices without being immersed in any of them, even great masters have struggled with the same issue. For instance, Lama Tsongkhapa, the founder of the Gelug order of Tibetan Buddhism, read many contradictory texts on the nature of emptiness that confused him more than they helped to lead him to realization. "It wasn't until he studied the profound teachings of the Indian sage Nāgārjuna, and then Candrakīrti, that Tsongkhapa discovered an explanation that was very clear and decisive," Genla says.

Besides advising people to avoid sectarianism but to still stick to one path, Genla offers yet another word of caution. "There are so many misrepresentations, you should be very careful," he explains. He then reiterates that practitioners should develop a solid base in the tradition that best resonates with them before they start comparing it with other schools. "The main thing is not the book; it is to develop a good heart and become a better person through practice." Genla says he is amazed that Western scientists and scholars haven't yet applied their research skills to testing this essential premise: that the root of increasing happiness and reducing suffering in life is cultivating a positive mind and reducing a negative mind. "The purpose of practice is to change your mind and to cultivate a good heart," he says. "The main thing is positive mental development."

Because of numerous requests from his students, Gen Lamrimpa returned to Seattle for a three-month visit in 1992-93, during which he gave teachings. He then traveled to Switzerland and Italy, and returned to India in time for the Kālacakra initiation in Gangtok, Sikkim. Since then he has remained in solitary meditation in Sikkim.

Chapter One
Introduction

THE SIGNIFICANCE OF COMPASSION AND INSIGHT

By meditating on emptiness one can sever the root of cyclic existence. This implies that if one meditates on emptiness with a spirit of emergence, one can eradicate the afflictive obscurations, and if this practice is motivated by a spirit of awakening, one can further eradicate the cognitive obscurations. In this way one can attain full awakening, the enlightenment of a *buddha*, which then provides the full capacity for utterly relieving the suffering of others and bringing them to a lasting state of well-being. Hence, the cultivation of the motivation is very important.

The initial intention is very important for any type of activity in which we may engage. For mundane activities, an ordinary intention is enough, but such a mundane motivation of simply getting the job done does not suffice for the type of activity we are discussing here. It is important to cultivate a special motivation. We must cultivate a wholesome motivation, and the most virtuous motivation we can cultivate is the one to dispel the suffering of others and to bring others to a state of well-being.

In fact, the revelation of the Buddha, including both the scriptures and insight, has compassion as its root. The teachings offered here are included in the Mahāyāna Dharma. In this context great compassion is indispensable. Compassion is a state of mind intent on protecting others from suffering. It is a priceless quality of awareness. If compassion fills one's own heart, one can bring others to a state of well-being and protect them from suffering. Moreover, if other people have compassion directed at oneself, this also makes them happier. One might say that compassion is the root of joy and happiness.

As an example, in your household, if you are a compassionate person, this brings happiness to the rest of the people in your family. Moreover, if all the members of a family have kind, compassionate natures, then in both hard times and good times, this quality of awareness brings about happiness for all of them. Taking a broader view, if the whole world were filled with compassionate people, there would be no question that happiness would reign.

One attains the full awakening of buddhahood exclusively by cultivating compassion and by following a path of compassion. This does not mean that compassion alone is sufficient, but rather that compassion is necessary; there is no spiritual path apart from the cultivation of compassion. Therefore, it is very important to cultivate the motivation of compassion, to yearn to free all sentient beings from suffering. With this motivation attend to the teachings on emptiness and then engage in the practice.

The *Questions of Ārya-Rāṣṭapāla Sūtra* (*Ārya-Rāṣṭapālaparipṛcchā-sūtra*) states that due to ignorance of emptiness, peace, and the unborn, sentient beings wander in the cycle of existence. The phrase emphasizes emptiness, because all phenomena, including oneself, are devoid of any inherent nature. In this context "peace" refers to freedom from conceptual elaboration, which entails grasping onto true existence. Finally, "the unborn" implies that in this sphere of freedom from conceptual elaboration, there is no arising, and since there is no arising, there is no cessation. This is the ultimate mode of all phenomena, but due to the ignorance of this reality, living beings wander in the cycle of existence. Because of our ignorance of how phenomena actually exist, we are not merely in the dark; rather, our false apprehension of how phenomena exist perpetuates our cycling in *saṃsāra*.

Thus, the passage paraphrased above illustrates the relationship between compassion and wisdom. The passage shows the *bodhisattva's* great compassion and the Buddha's analysis of the nature of existence. Having recognized how sentient beings suffer from confusion, the *bodhisattvas* and the *buddhas* have revealed numerous avenues of understanding for gaining realization of emptiness. In such a way, if one can gain a nonconceptual realization of emptiness, one can totally eliminate not only all mental afflictions, but also the impressions upon the mind from such afflictions.

Even if one does not have such a nonconceptual realization, one may have a conceptual realization of emptiness, in which one's experience of emptiness is mixed with a generic idea of emptiness. This too is said to be very beneficial. However, if one lacks any understanding or realization of emptiness, then all of one's other virtues—including compassion, generosity, moral discipline, patience, zeal, or meditative stabilization—are said to be blind.

In what sense are these virtues said to be blind? They do not provide a perception of one's actual goal in order to make the way clear. Just as a blind person cannot be a guide, in the same way, even if one is endowed with such virtues as great compassion or a spirit of awakening, if one lacks a realization of emptiness, one is not capable of being a guide for others or of effectively leading others from suffering. That is, one cannot totally eradicate others' suffering together with its roots and lead them to a lasting state of well-being. However, if a blind person has a guide, then he can be led to his desired destination.

Even someone with great compassion needs an understanding or realization of emptiness. The same holds true for the other five of the six perfections, namely generosity, ethical discipline, patience, zeal, and meditative stabilization. If one is lacking a realization of emptiness, these do not even get the name of "perfection." They are given that name only if they are conjoined with a realization of emptiness. The Tibetan term "perfection" (Tib. *pha rol tu phyin pa*) literally means "to go beyond," or "transcend." Thus, the perfection of wisdom is so called because it leads one beyond the cycle of existence to the transcendent state of liberation.

What are the benefits of transcending *saṃsāra*, this cycle of existence in which one is subject to birth, aging, sickness, and death? By transcending the cycle of existence you attain a state in which you are free from both birth and cessation. This is like escaping from the gravitational field of the earth in a spaceship. In short, the perfection of wisdom has extraordinary benefits to it.

Before gaining a nonconceptual realization of emptiness, if you can gain some sense of the nature of emptiness, it is like punching a hole in the bag of *saṃsāra*. You may not have burst it, but you have made it leak. Āryadeva, the great Indian philosopher, declared that if one even questions the true existence of reality, this shakes the foundations of *saṃsāra*. It is said that some people acquire great merit just by hearing the word "emptiness," due to their sensing the great meaning of this word. Thus, listening to teachings on emptiness can have great significance, so if you are looking for a meaningful essence, you can find it.

To give an analogy, if you are steadily traveling along a wrong path, you will continue on your way wholeheartedly as long as you cannot see another road. But if you hear that there is another road, then a doubt is sown in your mind, and gradually your perseverance in following the wrong road declines. The doubt will grow to a point where you think that this may not be the right road, and by the time you get to an intersection, you will be looking for another road. As soon as you find it you can totally change direction. To bring this analogy to the subject of this teaching, the wrong road is the path of ignorance and the correct road is the wisdom of emptiness. The reality of emptiness is really the essential criterion for whether your path is the right or the wrong one. This is why it is said that even having some uncertainty will wear *saṃsāra* ragged.

Even if one cultivates a spirit of awakening to a considerable extent, if one lacks a realization of emptiness, one cannot cut the root of *saṃsāra*. As long as one lacks that, one can never gain mastery over such things as birth, aging, sickness, and death. Therefore, the wisdom of realizing emptiness is something very precious.

SUITABLE TEACHERS AND STUDENTS FOR
TEACHINGS ON EMPTINESS

Who are the appropriate recipients for these teachings? To be an appropriate recipient, one needs quite a few qualities. First one needs to have faith in such teachings, and second, one must be certain about the fact that emptiness does not mean utter nonexistence. Third, when establishing the mode of existence of phenomena, one must recognize that activities, relationships, and functions occur even though phenomena are empty of inherent existence.

It is said that if one has these qualities, then it is appropriate to receive teachings on emptiness. An inappropriate recipient, for example, may be a person who thinks, "If I do not exist, then I do not accumulate *karma,* and since I do not accumulate *karma,* I do not have to experience the results of *karma.*" Quite to the contrary, it is necessary to assert the validity of the following statement in the context of the teachings on emptiness: While phenomena are empty of inherent nature, they do exist in a dependently related fashion, and therefore activities and functions can be established.

Nāgārjuna stated that anything that is fit to be empty of inherent existence is fit to have all qualities, while anything that is not fit to be empty is not fit to have any qualities. This means that if something is empty of inherent nature, then the

Four Noble Truths can definitely be established. If there were something not empty of inherent existence, then the Four Noble Truths could not be established.

I find that many Westerners are drawn to the topic of emptiness, and as this is the case it is important to recognize that emptiness does not mean utter nonexistence. Although things are empty, their relative functions are still valid. I will explain later on how things empty of inherent existence are fit to have functions and relationships, and how things not empty of inherent existence may not have such functions, qualities, or relationships.

It is very important, if you ever do teach emptiness, to make sure that the people you are teaching are free from the pitfall of thinking that since phenomena are empty of inherent existence they are therefore nonexistent, and that causal relationships don't hold. If you are not careful of that and teach people who would respond in that way, you would incur a downfall if you have taken the *bodhisattva* precepts. It is important to emphasize this point when giving teachings on emptiness. The reason for the seriousness of this issue is that if people infer that since phenomena are empty, they are therefore nonexistent, and that therefore there is no *karma*, such people undermine the very basis of their spiritual practice of cultivating the wholesome and avoiding the unwholesome.

Now that we have covered the qualifications of an appropriate recipient of the teachings on emptiness, the next question is, What are the qualities of the fully qualified recipient of teachings on emptiness? These are discussed in the text *A Guide to the Middle Way* (*Madhyamakāvatāra*) by Candrakīrti. There he says that one of the characteristics of a fully qualified recipient is that one repeatedly becomes thrilled by such teachings, such that tears may flow from gladness. Some people cry for joy when they gamble and win. Some people cry for joy when they win a gold trophy. Just so, Candrakīrti says that tears of joy may spontaneously flow and one's hair may stand on end when one hears the teachings on emptiness.

This indicates that there are seeds, or potentialities, present that stimulate the awareness of one's naturally abiding *buddha-nature*, and this means that you are fit to realize emptiness. Then Candrakīrti says that the teachings on emptiness should be offered to such recipients.

Candrakīrti goes on to say that in order to meditate on emptiness in this and in future lives it is necessary to cultivate certain cooperative conditions that would facilitate such practice. For example, it is important not to be afflicted with poverty. It is difficult to meditate if you don't have enough to eat. To avoid poverty in future lives, engage in generosity, for the karmic result of generosity is the absence of poverty. In order to continue the practice in future lives, it is important to have a rebirth in a fortunate realm of existence. For this, one must cultivate ethical discipline. In order to be led by a spiritual mentor who will continue to guide one in one's practice, it is necessary to cultivate patience. Also, in order to have the proper incentive in future lives, one should cultivate a like cause in this life, namely enthusiasm. And the same holds true for the cultivation of meditative stabilization. These are all understood as sowing the seeds to produce conducive circumstances so that one will carry on with the practice in future lives. In order to carry the practice to its culmination, which is attaining the full awakening of a *buddha*, cultivating these practices is indispensable. By cultivating generosity and so forth, one paves the way for future lives in which one continues such practices. Moreover, this manner of cultivation enhances one's practice in this lifetime.

PROVISIONAL AND DEFINITIVE TEACHINGS WITHIN BUDDHISM

There are different lineages and traditions within classical Indian Buddhism regarding the teachings on emptiness. Also, within Tibet in the last millennium or so there have been a variety of ways of teaching emptiness. Among the *sūtras* of the Buddha there are many that are regarded as provisional, while other *sūtras* are definitive. The criterion for distinguishing between provisional and definitive *sūtras*, according to the Prāsaṅgika system, is that those *sūtras* whose chief and explicit topic is emptiness are regarded as definitive *sūtras*, while those *sūtras* whose explicit topic is conventional truth are regarded as provisional. Therefore, emptiness itself is said to be the definitive meaning. And conventional truth is said to be provisional.

Why is emptiness said to be definitive? The reason for this is that for the mind that nonconceptually realizes emptiness, the mode of appearance of emptiness and its mode of existence are in accord with each other. However, for all conventional truths, the way things exist and the way they appear are incongruent. How so? For a sentient being, that is for anyone who is not a *buddha*, things appear as if they were truly existent, whereas their actual mode of existence is that they are not truly existent. Thus such phenomena are called provisional, because they cannot be accepted at face value.

THE LINEAGE OF THESE TEACHINGS

The Buddha gave many teachings concerning ultimate and conventional truths, so these many, diverse teachings can easily be misinterpreted. Aware of this danger, the Buddha prophesied that 400 years after his *parinirvāṇa*, there would appear in the south of India a monk whose name would begin with the word Nāga. This person, he said, would accurately distinguish between the definitive and the provisional teachings of the Buddha.

Ācārya Nāgārjuna appeared in fulfillment of this prophesy, and he composed many treatises and texts, the principal one being *A Fundamental Treatise on the Middle Way* (*Mūlamadhymakakārikā*), whose subject matter is emptiness. After him came the Indian *paṇḍit* Buddhapālita, who composed a commentary to that treatise. After him, another Indian *paṇḍit* by the name of Bhāvaviveka concluded that Buddhapālita had misinterpreted Nāgārjuna's treatise, so he composed his own commentary, thereby laying the foundation for the Svātantrika

Madhyamaka school. Bhāvaviveka's thesis is that phenomena do not exist by their own nature, but they do exist by their own characteristics.

Thereafter, Ācārya Candrakīrti drew the conclusion that Buddhapālita's commentary was actually sound, and it was Bhāvaviveka who had misinterpreted Nāgārjuna's teachings. Candrakīrti then composed his own commentary and thereby laid the foundation for the Prāsaṅgika Madhyamaka school. Candrakīrti states that if phenomena were to exist by their own characteristics, they would be incapable of functioning.

Centuries later, the Indian *paṇḍit* Atiśa confirmed that Candrakīrti had presented the only appropriate interpretation of Nāgārjuna's thought, and the Tibetan sage Tsongkhapa concurred, saying that Nāgārjuna showed the way out of ignorance, and Candrakīrti identified the erroneous interpretation of Bhāvaviveka while revealing the true import of Nāgārjuna's teachings. Tsongkhapa gained a direct vision of Mañjuśrī, and on many occasions he conversed with Mañjuśrī to clarify points concerning emptiness. Eventually Tsongkhapa gained direct realization of emptiness, which he said resulted from the kindness of his gurus.

It is said that most of the realizations of the *bodhisattva* grounds and paths leading to full enlightenment arise in direct dependence upon the blessings of the guru. When Tsongkhapa speaks of the kindness of his gurus, he is referring chiefly to his own principal spiritual mentor, Rendawa. Such statements about the kindness of the guru are very common in Buddhism, and they are designed to counter any lingering remnant of conceit. In a similar fashion, Śāntideva comments in his treatise *A Guide to the Bodhisattva Way of Life* (*Bodhicaryāvatāra* I: 2):

> There is nothing here that has not been said before, nor do I have any skill in composition. Thus, I have no concern for the welfare of others, and I have composed this solely to season my own mind.

Tsongkhapa writes of a dream he had in which Nāgārjuna and his spiritual sons appeared, including Āryadeva,

Buddhapālita, Bhāvaviveka, and Candrakīrti. In Tsongkhapa's dream, those five *paṇḍits* were discussing emptiness and the way phenomena exist as dependently related events. After their discussion, Buddhapālita took a text and he placed it on Tsongkhapa's head while blessing him. When Tsongkhapa woke up in the morning, all his qualms and uncertainties about the topic of emptiness were immediately dispelled. While reading Buddhapālita's commentary, the meaning became totally clear and he gained a direct realization of emptiness.

Given this discussion of the various lineages raises the question: Is there any benefit in studying the other schools, since Candrakīrti, Atiśa, and Tsongkhapa all accepted the Prāsaṅgika view? Candrakīrti commented that one does not gain a realization simply by studying but only through long familiarization with the teachings on emptiness. Even if one is extremely erudite that will not suffice. This being the case, if one studies all the different schools of Buddhist thought, including the Vaibhāṣika, Sautrāntika, Yogācāra, Svātantrika Madhyamaka, and Prāsaṅgika Madhyamaka, one sees how each system grapples with reality. Then one can investigate each school's limitations and fallacies in a progressive fashion. This method is a very effective means for approaching the insight revealed in the Prāsaṅgika interpretation. By clearly distinguishing one school from the others, great clarity of understanding arises, and one can avoid many errors in understanding. My own teacher Gen Nyima said that if one is supported by a strong collection of merit, the realization of emptiness is easy, but otherwise such emptiness is extremely difficult. So I would encourage you to study very broadly if you can, for this will give rise to a high degree of clarity of understanding. This is the advantage of great erudition.

Even without such erudition, one may realize emptiness chiefly by the force of one's acquaintance with it in previous lives, but if one then tries to teach this to others, one may easily mislead them. However, if one teaches emptiness out of both one's own realization and a sound theoretical understanding, one would not conflate different interpretations of these teachings. Thus, one's explanations would be clear and unconfused.

For example, if you had gained a realization of emptiness but were not very erudite, you might pick up a *sūtra* that accords with the Yogācāra system, which asserts the existence of a total-ground consciousness. Even though you had a realization of emptiness, you might conclude that such a consciousness exists because it is posited in that *sūtra*. But later on, you might read a Prāsaṅgika text that refutes the existence of a total-ground consciousness. Based upon the authority of the great *paṇḍit* Asaṅga, you would conclude that such consciousness does exist, but based upon the authority of Candrakīrti, you would refute it, for he stated that many absurd consequences follow if such a consciousness is posited. To fully understand this seeming contradiction, study is important.

Candrakīrti did not have higher realization than Asaṅga or Maitreya, but asserted that the teachings on the total-ground consciousness are only provisional. Such teachings may be helpful for particular people at a particular phase in their spiritual development, but they are not actually in accord with reality. Buddha Śākyamuni himself at times stated that a personal identity exists, while at other times he said that it does not exist. On those occasions when he said that a personal identity exists, he did so for a special purpose, because in particular cases this teaching would be most effective for leading others out of their delusions. Nevertheless, such statements are not finally in accordance with reality, which is to say they are not definitive.

The lineage of the present teaching comes from Atiśa, Tsongkhapa, and a line of lamas of his lineage. I believe that Tsongkhapa and the entire succession of teachers following him, up to and including the lama from whom I received teachings on emptiness, all gained realization of emptiness. My own teacher Shako Khen Rinpoche, also widely known as Gen Nyima, was regarded as the finest teacher of emptiness among all the great monastic universities of Ganden, Drepung, and

Sera. He was so called by a great contemplative and scholar named Debokhyil Rinpoche (Tib. De bo 'khyil rin po che), and His Holiness the Dalai Lama also commented that he was the foremost of teachers of emptiness. Gen Nyima's teacher, whose name was Tongpön Rinpoche, was a great contemplative, as was his teacher. He was said to have memorized all 108 volumes of the entire collected teachings of the Buddha, while my teacher memorized all 36 volumes of Tsongkhapa's teachings and those of his great disciples Khedrub Je and Gyaltsab Je. So there is a great blessing in this lineage. The method of teaching of this lineage is also extremely good. My own teacher taught closely in accordance with the teachings of Nāgārjuna, Candrakīrti, and Tsongkhapa. Until me, there is a great blessing in this lineage, though I myself have very little to offer. Nevertheless, for about twenty years I have been pondering and meditating upon emptiness with great enthusiasm.

SCRIPTURAL SOURCES FOR THESE TEACHINGS

Śāntideva states in his text *A Guide to the Bodhisattva Way of Life* that the causes for joy are few, whereas the causes for discontent and suffering are many. Indeed, the causes for happiness and joy are very rare, and naturally there are many, many causes for suffering. It is also said that one has to learn to distinguish between virtue and nonvirtue, for one does not simply know this instinctively. It is important to learn this distinction because virtue is the cause of well-being, while nonvirtue is the cause of misery. However, the full extent of the relationships between virtuous and nonvirtuous actions and their consequences is only taught by a *buddha*. It is also said that the relationship between actions and their results, or the law of *karma*, is very subtle and difficult to realize, even more so than emptiness. Furthermore, only a fully awakened being is able to know and to reveal infallibly in detail the relationship between actions and their results. Unfortunately, the appearance of a fully awakened being in the world is very rare, and moreover, it is very difficult to have the fortune to take birth during a time when a *buddha* is living. In light of these statements it seems almost impossible to engage in virtue; that is, the occasional virtue is extremely rare.

It is even more rare to have the opportunity to hear teachings that allow one to cultivate the realization of emptiness, which is the direct antidote for cutting the root of suffering. Thus, we are very fortunate to have this opportunity to have teachings on emptiness, and it is important to cherish it. This means one should cherish it by listening to the teachings, reflecting upon them, and meditating on them. It is insufficient simply to hear teachings on emptiness; it is even insufficient to gain a realization of emptiness once. What one needs to do is gain a realization and then familiarize oneself more and more with that realization in order to utterly cut the root of suffering.

By and large, we may only concern ourselves with affairs that pertain to this life; however, the meditation on emptiness is something that we plan to do from lifetime to lifetime. Listening to teachings on emptiness in this lifetime and reflecting on them ripens our mind-streams, which facilitates such realizations in future lives. It is very important to engage in the investigation of emptiness on a continuing basis. One may gain a sense of understanding of what it is about fairly rapidly, but it is important not to be satisfied with that. Rather, one should continue to probe more and more deeply because a deep realization is not so easily won.

This discussion of emptiness is based on the general format of a text by Tsongkhapa called *An Elucidation of the Meaning of the Middle Way* (Tib. *dBu ma dgongs pa rab gsal*). In this text Tsongkhapa comments on *A Guide to the Middle Way* by Candrakīrti, which is one of Candrakīrti's commentaries to Nāgārjuna's *Fundamental Treatise on the Middle Way*.

The term "Middle Way" can refer either to emptiness, as the referent of that word, or it may refer to the teachings on that reality. In the title of *A Guide to the Middle Way* this term refers to the teachings on this subject, and this is also true for the title of Tsongkhapa's text *An Elucidation of the Meaning of the Middle Way*. On the other hand, when this word appears in the title of Nāgārjuna's *Fundamental Treatise on the Middle Way*, it refers to the reality of the Middle Way. Candrakīrti's text *A Guide to the Middle Way* is so called because it elucidates the meaning of Nāgārjuna's treatise with respect to both its profound and vast aspects.

Tsongkhapa's text *An Elucidation of the Meaning of the Middle Way* discusses the object to be refuted as one seeks to understand emptiness. He quotes the "Wisdom" chapter of Śāntideva's *A Guide to the Bodhisattva Way of Life* (IX: 139), which states, "Without detecting an imagined thing, its nonexistence is not apprehended." In other words, if one does not recognize the misleading mode of appearance of phenomena—misleading in the sense that things appear as if they were truly existent—it is not possible to realize the absence of true existence. In order to ascertain the object that is to be refuted, it is necessary to identify the way in which we grasp onto true existence. Thus, it is necessary to identify the object to be refuted.

An Elucidation of the Meaning of the Middle Way asserts the manner in which phenomena exist purely as conceptual designations. What needs to be understood is that phenomena exist by the force of conceptual designations. The refutation of the true existence of phenomena implies that they exist in a dependent and related fashion. What is the chief manner in which phenomena are dependent on other phenomena? The chief dependence is upon conceptual designation. By realizing that phenomena exist by the force of conceptual designation, it is easy to ascertain the nature of grasping onto true existence.

There are two parts to the following presentation: 1) the manner in which phenomena are established as being conceptually designated, and 2) the manner of grasping onto true existence.

Chapter Two
How Phenomena Are Established as Being Conceptually Designated

Tsongkhapa begins his explanation on the Middle Way by citing the Buddha's assertion that everything in the world has been brought forth not by a divine creator but by the power of conceptual designation. The Buddha also asserted that the world has come forth by ignorance, and if this is true, then phenomena do not exist apart from conceptual designation. Āryadeva states in his text *The Four Hundred Stanzas* (*Catuḥśatakaṭika*) that in the absence of ignorance other mental afflictions such as attachment do not arise. And those phenomena which are designated by conceptualization—here conceptualization refers to ignorance—are not real. He goes on to state that all phenomena in the cycle of existence follow from the activation of ignorance. These phenomena cannot exist in the absence of conceptualization. Rather, they exist in dependence upon conditions and are as deceptive as a snake that appears on the basis of a striped rope. These are all themes developed by Tsongkhapa.

THE FUSION OF WORD-BASED IDEAS WITH EXPERIENCE-BASED IDEAS

To understand how phenomena are dependent upon conceptual designation, it is first necessary to identify what is meant by conceptual designations (Tib. *rtog btags*), imputed entities (Tib. *btags yod*), and conceptualization (Tib. *rtog pa*) itself. Generally speaking, conceptualization is a type of cognition that apprehends objects by way of generic ideas.

There are two ways of understanding conceptualization. On the one hand, it may be understood a compulsive thought process that is able to fuse, or integrate word-based ideas (Tib. *sgra spyi*) and experience-based ideas (Tib. *don spyi*). Let us use an example to understand the term "word-based idea." In Tibet there is a region called Phari. Purely on the basis of a verbal description, there can arise in the mind an idea of that part of Tibet. On the one hand you can have an idea of Phari based on a verbal description of that part of Tibet, and on the other hand you can go to that region without knowing it is called Phari, and you may form an idea of that area based on your own experience. In the former case, you acquire a word-based idea of that region, and in the latter case you acquire an experience-based idea. The former is based purely on a verbal description without any experience, and the other is based on experience without any verbal designation.

Khedrub Je, one of the two principal disciples of Tsong-khapa, asserts that a word-based idea need not be classified separately from an experience-based idea, for they are both generic ideas. However, in his text *A Commentary on Verifying Cognition (Pramāṇavārtika)*—a text largely concerned with logic and epistemology—Dharmakīrti states that there are two types of conceptualization: one that is associated with a name, and another that is associated with reality.

For example, in conceiving of something like the Seattle Space Needle, an image of that tower appears to the mind. The image of the Space Needle that appears to the conceptual mind is said to be the generic idea of the Space Needle, and we say that mind apprehends the Space Needle itself and not the generic idea of the tower. In short, the generic idea of the Space Needle *appears* to that conceptual mind, but it apprehends the Space Needle.

Merely because something appears to a conceptual mind does not necessarily imply that the conceptual mind apprehends that appearance. Both types of ideas appear to us, the verbal idea and the generic idea. We can say that to the conceptual mind that apprehends the Space Needle there arises the appearance of the Space Needle, and we can say that the appearance of that Space Needle is a generic idea of the Space Needle.

It is very important to understand what is meant by the generic idea. If one fails to grasp that, then the references to the realization of emptiness by means of a generic idea will be meaningless. The wisdom that realizes personal identity-lessness focuses upon the self, the "I," and it apprehends it as not truly existent. The ignorance that reifies the self also focuses on the "I," but it falsely apprehends it as truly existent. Thus, there are two types of mutually incompatible cognitions: first, grasping onto true existence of the self, and second, the realization of emptiness with regard to the self. Even though they focus on the same thing, their modes of apprehension are mutually incompatible. If one does not understand what is meant by a generic image, the path to understanding this line of reasoning is blocked.

We can say that the generic idea appears to the conceptual mind, and we also say with regard to the conceptualization of the Space Needle, that the Space Needle appears to that conceptual mind. To the conceptual mind that apprehends a Space Needle, both the generic idea and the Space Needle appear. But now you may ask, "What does this conceptual mind apprehend? Does it apprehend the generic idea of the Space Needle?" The answer is no. What does it apprehend? It apprehends the Space Needle. In contrast, you should remember that for sensory cognitions, such as auditory or visual cognition, whatever is apprehended by the cognition is the same as what appears to it.

THE FUSION OF THE OBJECT
WITH THE GENERIC IDEA OF THE OBJECT

Now we come to the second technical definition of conceptualization. Once again, it is the same concept, but here we give a different interpretation of the two entities that are fused: not a verbal idea and an experiential idea, but rather the object and the generic idea. From this point of view, conceptualization is defined as a compulsive cognition that can fuse together the object and the generic idea of the object (Tib. *don spyi 'dres par 'dzin pa'i rtogs pa*).

The point is that conceptualization has the capacity for fusing together the object and the generic idea of the object, without clearly distinguishing between the two. It is generally said that conceptualization is a deceptive cognition, because it mistakes the generic idea for the actual object. Appearances arise to the conceptual mind, which has the ability to distinguish one entity from another. It is also said that for any conceptualization, phenomena do not appear as vividly as they occur for perception. Appearances clearly arise only to nonconceptual cognition. When one gains a nonconceptual, or perceptual, realization of emptiness, one's experience of emptiness is not filtered through generic ideas. This entails an absence of a generic idea and an absence of conceptualization.

To understand the manner in which phenomena exist as conceptual designations let's take an example. Imagine three rooms that are virtually identical in every way, including their the size, the location of windows, shape, and so forth. You have these rooms, but they have not been labeled yet. Generally, you know that one of them is going to be your kitchen, one of them is going to be your dining room, and one of them will be your bedroom. But you have not yet decided which is to be which. Among those three empty and identical rooms, is there a kitchen or not? No labels have been applied; there has been no conceptual designation yet. Here are some questions to consider: Is there a kitchen because every house has a kitchen? Is there no kitchen because no room has the things that make it a kitchen? Is there a kitchen because of its structural form? When does a kitchen first come into existence?

In the architect's mind there is the idea that there is to be a kitchen. But prior to the actual designation of which room is to be the kitchen, a kitchen is not to be found in any of those rooms. But when you hear the assertion that there is no kitchen in any of these three rooms, you can ask, "Wasn't there a plan for a kitchen?" Although there was a plan for a kitchen, it is not identifiable among those three rooms. There is no way by looking at these three rooms to identify any one as a kitchen. At that point, if you ask if any of those rooms is a basis of designation for the kitchen, the answer is no.

It is said that the designated object and the basis of designation are of the same nature. When you say that two things are of the same nature, it means that they invariably exist together: in the absence of one, the other cannot be present. If the basis of designation were to exist before the designated object came into being, they would not be of the same nature. Even if you fit a particular room out with a refrigerator, stove, and so on, that does not make it a kitchen. For example, it could merely be a storage room.

Before there is the designation of a room as a kitchen, no kitchen exists. You may have the original general plan to have a kitchen, a dining room, and a bedroom in your house, but they come into existence only when you designate them as such: This is my kitchen, this is the dining room, and this is the bedroom. From that point on these three rooms do exist. Then it is for the rest of the world to acknowledge their existence. Whether or not the kitchen exists in this case is purely a matter of convention: it is first so designated, then it is accepted as such by others. By stating that something is conceptually designated, this implies an agreement or an assertion.

As you may notice, there are two designators here: one is the label and the other is conceptualization. By identifying a room as the basis of designation of a kitchen, the kitchen is so designated, whether or not the parts or appliances we associate with the kitchen are there. The basis of designation of a kitchen comes into existence simultaneously with the designation of the kitchen.

For one thing to be the basis of designation for a designated object, simply seeing that basis should enable a knowledgeable person to recognize the designated object. Any portion of a basis of designation does not necessarily suffice to be the basis of designation for the designated object. For instance, the head, from the neck up, may not be called the basis of designation for the person, because merely seeing the head does not necessarily lead to the recognition of that person. If you beheaded someone and stuck the head on a pole, it would simply be wrong to say, "This is a person." The head itself does not arouse the recognition of a person. The basis of designation is something that clarifies the designated object.

So we can see there are three things involved in this process:

1. The basis of designation (Tib. *gdags gzhi*), which is something that appears to any of the six senses.
2. The designator, which is of two types: (a) the conceptualizing mind and (b) the conventional labeling and agreement on that labeling.
3. The designated object (Tib. *btags chos*).

One should note that the combination of the first two elements leads to the third element of the process.

Let's take another example: This body and mind are the basis of designation of a person. The person is the designated object that is designated upon this particular basis of designation. The designator is of two types, the conventional labeling, or agreement, and the conceptualization. In dependence upon the three—the basis of designation, the designated object, and the designator—the person exists. When any of those three—the basis of designation, the designated object, or the designator—is missing, one cannot establish the existence of a person. Therefore it is said that all phenomena are merely conceptual designations. When we say that things are conceptually designated, this is an assertion, or an agreement.

I suggest an exercise to familiarize yourself with this. As you look around at different objects and events, mentally comment, "This is simply a conceptual designation." As you do so, try to identify the basis of designation of these various objects that you identify, and see how you label things that have no label in themselves.

One might agree that all things are conceptually designated, but an even stronger statement is that phenomena are *merely* conceptual designations. We should check this out for ourselves to see whether it holds true. As we gain clarity there, it will be somewhat easier to identify how ignorance operates.

For there to be a basis of designation, there must necessarily be something that is cognized (Tib. *dmigs pa*) as well as a referent object of that cognition (Tib. *dmigs yul*). In addition, there must be an awareness that is the simple cognition of the basis of designation (Tib. *dmigs mkhan*).

If something is a referent object of the mere "I," it must also be a basis of designation of the mere "I." If something is a basis of designation, it is necessarily an object of the cognizing awareness that apprehends the basis of designation.

If something is a referent object, it is not necessarily a basis of designation. If something is the referent object of oneself, the referent object of the mind that apprehends the self is identical with the basis of designation of the self. But if something is a referent object, it need not be a basis of designation. For example, "I" is a referent object, but "I" is not a basis of designation. If something is a referent object it is necessarily an object, and if something is a basis of designation it is necessarily an object.

If grasping onto true existence arises, other mental afflictions do not necessarily ensue from it. However, if any mental affliction such as attachment or hostility does arise, it is necessarily preceded by such reification, and other conditions such as a referent object and a cognizing awareness must also be present. Objects of attachment include other individuals and oneself. Focusing on oneself might give rise to self-centeredness or to self-contempt, and both occur due to one's previous habitual tendencies.

I have heard that here in the West it is quite common for people to feel self-contempt and hatred toward themselves, and sometimes even to wish to harm themselves. People may disparage themselves, thinking, "I don't engage in spiritual practice very well." In fact, such self-disparagement, or self-contempt, is not opposite to self-centeredness. Rather, such aversion arises upon the very basis of self-centeredness. If you wish to overcome self-centeredness, you can do so by cherishing others. When you are consumed with self-contempt or self-disparagement, there is no room for cherishing others. Rather, you are too concerned with yourself alone. Great compassion counteracts self-centeredness, and it does so through the cultivation of a sense of cherishing others.

We are presented with a choice as to the center of our priorities: will we be centered on ourselves, on our own well-being, or will our priorities and concerns be centered on the well-being of others? The former is called self-centeredness and the latter is called cherishing others. Great compassion involves cherishing others. Moreover, if we fail to make this distinction and erroneously assume that by means of self-contempt and self-deprecation we will overcome self-centeredness and open the way to altruism, to compassion and so forth, we are actually blocking the path to cultivating a spirit of awakening. To counter such self-deprecation we should focus on the reality that we are capable beings. If we really apply ourselves, nothing is impossible for us. If we apply ourselves in accordance with our own abilities, we can accomplish whatever we set out to do, including both mundane activities and spiritual ventures.

It is different for animals: animals lack the intelligence to discern what to follow and what to avoid. For them there are severe limitations. Even though some animals may seem to be very clever in some respects, they are still hindered by stupidity. For example, we may think that dogs are very clever, but without being trained by human beings, they are not clever at all.

To apply our intelligence to identifying the designated object, we must understand what is meant by saying two things are of the same nature. First, they have to be distinct, or in other words, they cannot be identical. Second, the perception that sees them must not see them as being of a distinct nature, but must see them indivisibly. Such things are said to be of the same nature.

If you have identified something as a basis of designation, it needs to be something that implies the designated object for the mind that apprehends it. For example, impermanence is designated on the basis of my hand. The basis of designation of impermanence and the basis of designation of hand are of the same nature. But the attitudes, or the ways of thinking, with regard to the basis of designation as something impermanent and as a hand are quite distinct. The basis of designation of something that is impermanent has to be something that is subject to change. But the basis of designation for a hand must be a limb of some person or other being. Although those two bases of designation of an impermanent object and a hand are of the same nature, the ways in which the designated objects are brought forth are different. It may also happen that one name may be used as a designation for two totally different things, or totally different things may be designated with the same term. One person may have three different names, but there is only one basis of designation for all three.

The basis of designation is not of the same nature as the generic idea. A pot exists in dependence upon the generic idea of a pot. And the existence of the generic idea of the pot is dependent upon the pot. As this is true of the pot, so is this true of the basis of designation of the pot. The basis of designation of the pot does not exist independently of the generic idea of the pot. The generic idea of the pot does not exist independently of the basis of designation of the pot. But the two are not of the same nature. It would seem that when you gaze at the pot, what actually appears to your visual perception is merely the basis of designation of the pot. But, by the appearance of the basis of designation of the pot, we say a pot appears to the mind. If the two were of the same nature—that is, if the generic idea of the pot and the basis of designation of the pot were of the same nature—then the generic idea of the pot would have to exist in the basis of designation. But the generic idea exists only in here in the mind, which is where the reification of the self occurs.

We have this convention, don't we, of outer and inner? In terms of our conventions we say that the hand is out there. We don't say the hand is in here. You must have already had an experience of a hand which provides you with a generic idea of the hand, and when you see this appearance which corresponds to your generic idea, based upon your previous experience, you recall your generic idea and identify this is as a hand. First of all you have to see it in order for there to be a generic idea in the conceptual mind. You may have seen a hand in January, and then if you see this hand in March you say, "This is a hand." What you recall is nothing more than your January experience. In reality, the hand you recall from January has undergone a lot of changes in the meantime.

This is one reason why such phenomena are said to be deceptive. This would not be the case if they were truly existent. Taking phenomena that have form as a basis, their existence depends upon the visual perception and conceptual designation of a sentient being. For the nonconceptual mind, there may be a visual awareness of a hand, but the visual awareness is immediately followed by a conceptual awareness that makes distinctions. But the visual awareness, which is nonconceptual, is not able to make distinctions. It is said that for a nonconceptual cognition of a hand, the hand and everything that is of the same nature as the hand all appear to it. It is said that for such an awareness, as soon as you see the hand, you see its various qualities.

Let us now return to the topic of conceptualization and recall its definition as a compulsive cognition that can fuse together the object and the generic idea of the object. In this definition, what is a compulsive cognition, and what is the object? Taking the example of a conceptualization of a vase, the vase is the object. And the compulsive cognition of the vase apprehends that object as if it were fused with the generic idea of the vase. Conceptualization apprehends its object in dependence upon a generic idea, and it is called a compulsive cognition because it is a discursive process that distinguishes one thing from another. A nonconceptual awareness of a vase, in contrast, apprehends the vase, but it does not think "This is a vase."

The Tibetan verb "to designate" or "to impute" (Tib. *btags*) also has the connotation of "to bind" or "to tie," and in both cases this implies doing something to an object that wasn't already there from its own side. For example, you may tie a rope around a dog's neck in order fasten it to a tree. In that case, you are doing something to the dog that is not already there from its own side. You are adding more to its situation. Another important Tibetan term, "false superimposition" (Tib. *sgro btags pa*), also implies the imputation of something that is not there from its own side. The etymology of this Tibetan term is "fastening a feather," referring to attaching a feather on the end of an arrow. So whenever the terms "designate," "impute," and "superimpose" are used in this discussion, they all indicate the process of adding something that was not already there.

CONVENTIONAL AGREEMENT

As I mentioned previously, a conceptual designation entails a conventional agreement. The scriptural basis for this assertion is found in the Buddha's words, "That which the world asserts to be existent, I too assert to be existent, and that which the world asserts to be nonexistent, I too assert to be nonexistent." Thus, the assertion entails a conventional agreement. Such a process of agreement, or in fact the very term of "designation" or "imputation," implicitly denies inherent existence.

The Madhyamaka position is not simply that phenomena are conceptually designated, but that they are *merely* conceptual designations, and the implication of the term "merely" (Tib. *tsam*) in this context is that phenomena have no real existence apart from the process of conceptual designation. Nevertheless, doesn't it seem that things still appear to the mind, whether or not we designate them? Don't phenomena seem to have some kind of power in and of themselves? Isn't it simply counterintuitive to say that things are merely conceptual designations? So on what grounds is this assertion made?

In fact, to establish the existence of any phenomena, we do need a basis of designation. A sprout, for example, is not merely a conceptual designation in the sense of being a figment of our imaginations. If things were merely conceptual designations, then we could say fire is water, just by choosing to designate it as such. For example, in America we do not assert that *lagpas* exist. People in America do not believe in *lagpas*, so they don't exist in America. However, not everybody agrees with this. The Tibetans believe in *lagpas* [the word *lagpa* is Tibetan for hand].

As another example, there are apparently some people in a certain part of Tibet who call the eye (Tib. *mig*) "ear" (Tib. *a mchog*) and the ear "eye." In Tibetan one synonym for a human being is simply "biped" (Tib. *rkang gnyis*), for instance when referring to the Buddha as the "King of Bipeds." In this manner, one entity may have numerous names. On the other hand, many things can have the same name. An example of this would be the term *vajra*. The realization of emptiness is sometimes called *vajra*, but a scepter is called a *vajra*, a diamond is called a *vajra*, and a thunderbolt is also called a *vajra*.

Within a specific linguistic context, the labels must not be mixed up and everything that is identified must be labeled. If there is no label, then one will not be able to establish the functions of the unlabeled entities. Imagine one person who knows eighteen languages: he knows eighteen different labels for each thing, and he participates in eighteen conventional agreements, and by this participatory agreement is able to establish all of those things in any of these languages. Other people who do not know so many languages don't know all the terms that he does. Nevertheless, they too have designated the objects in their own way. The people and the linguist are alike insofar as he has conceptually designated the objects and they too have conceptually designated them. Our ability to establish a function, or an activity, of a certain object or entity comes purely from the power of conventional agreement. It does not come from the object's own side.

If you ask, "Is this a hand?" then the very clear accurate answer would be, "This is *called* a hand." If you counter this by saying: "Isn't this a hand?" then the realistic answer would be, "This is the *basis of designation* of a hand." Such a response is equally applicable to everything else. If you think or say about everything, "This is called this, this is called that," then by doing so, you mute the suggestion of inherent existence. We can call this a hand, and we can also say that it is the object designated on the basis of designation of a hand. We can also say that it is a basis of designation of a hand. In dependence upon this basis of designation we can impute many things: we can impute upon this the impermanence of the hand, the knowable objects of the hand, or many things that are synonymous with those knowable objects. For instance, if we are concerned with the outside we can designate skin, while if we are concerned with the inside, we can designate veins or arteries or bones, and so forth. What we have here is simply a whole collection of stuff.

In Madhyamaka teachings we encounter the statements that phenomena are "originally pure" of inherent existence (Tib. *gdod ma nas zhi ba*), "naturally liberated," (Tib. *rang bzhin gyis mya ngan las 'das pa*), and "naturally unestablished in reality" (Tib. *rang bzhin gyis ma grub pa*). Whether we want to say that things are pleasant or unpleasant, they are merely imputed as such. For example, if there is some disease in your hand, and you subject that disease to Madhyamaka analysis, then it cannot be found to exist from its own side any more than your hand can. It seems that in the process of conceptual designation we are really loading attributes onto things, which do not belong there by themselves. It is as though we are forcing things upon objects, and by using a hundred different languages to do so, we are overburdening them with all these designations and imputations. So if we ask, "How does a certain phenomenon exist?" the answer is that it is established by the power of consent. It thus seems that when something is conceptually designated, it is there, whereas if it is not conceptually designated, it is not there.

CAN WE ESTABLISH THINGS WITHOUT REFERRING TO THEM?

We can point a finger to the things we see and hear and so designate them. But can we establish something that does not appear to anyone's sense faculties, to things that lie outside anyone's experience? If we refer to a flower that we don't see, we have already conceptually designated it. Can we refer to something without designating or naming it?

How does it work for animals? They may not verbally designate things, and they may not use labels, but nevertheless, even wild animals designate phenomena. An animal, for instance, may come to a stream and experience an appearance of the water, which is impressed upon its awareness. And when that animal later on experiences thirst, then that generic idea of water will come to the animal's mind and it will seek out water. An animal having this generic idea of water may encounter a mirage of water and because of the similarity of what is being perceived and the preceding generic idea of water, the animal may go after the mirage.

Imagine that a number of years ago somebody looked through a telescope and saw something and labeled it as the planet Neptune, and not just as a speck of light. At that time the label Neptune was fresh, but even prior to that, he saw something. The crux of the matter is not even whether *we* saw something there or not. There is no guarantee that there are not some forms of sentient beings on Neptune or other sentient beings who might perceive it in some way. If one attains a very high degree of extrasensory perception (Tib. *mngon shes*), one can see objects at a distance of at least 500 *yojanas* [one *yojana* = approximately eight miles or five kilometers], including even very minute particles. With even more advanced extrasensory perception, it is possible to see all the atoms within a galaxy. But it is a little bit difficult for us to understand that type of clairvoyance. When one starts to utilize the power of the mind, one begins to see many facets of reality freshly that are not witnessed by most people. This is something that we can confirm by means of meditation; it definitely happens. Likewise, this is true of extrasensory perception: it can be cultivated; it can be attained. For example, very subtle karmic interrelationships are probably not evident to anyone besides *āryas*, superior beings who have gained a perceptual realization of emptiness. However, it is said that some spirits known as *pretas*—and these are by no means highly realized—perceive certain karmic relationships between actions and their results.

The Madhyamaka statement that all phenomena exist merely as conceptual designations may be rephrased in the following way: "For me, all phenomena exist merely as conceptual designations. All seen and unseen phenomena belong to this category." However, if one counters that statement with the question, "Are all possible phenomena designated by me?" then the answer is no. In order to bring forth a conceptual designation, one needs to bring together the basis of designation and the designated object. However, one can still say, "With respect to me all phenomena exist merely as conceptual designations," because this merely means that they are fit to be designated.

We need to make a distinction between conceptually designating something and knowing something. Let's take as an example education, from kindergarten up to the last year of doctoral studies. The entire course of the training has already been designated. Now if we ask whether a child who is just entering kindergarten has already conceptually designated all the subjects leading up to the doctoral degree, we would have to say that the child has not conceptually designated them; they are yet to be conceptually known by the child. But what is meant by the statement, "the child has yet to conceptually know them"? It means that the child is not yet able to do this on its own; the child has to gradually learn to do this. As the child hears, "This is called this, that is called that," and so forth, the child will pick up the designations and accept them with everyone else. As the child conceptually learns such terms, the child learns in accordance with the conceptual designations that have been made during its education. In contrast, when one first makes a conceptual designation one can do so with the utmost freedom. We must make such a distinction between these two situations.

How does a newborn infant make conceptual designations? I doubt that it would do so in accord with its modes of designation in a previous life, but this is not certain. I suspect it would make conceptual designations as animals do. Appearances would occur to the infant, and these would lead to generic ideas in the child's mind-stream, even before the infant is articulate. In the meantime, the baby would understand things in accordance with its own generic ideas, and would know that it likes this but does not like that, without having labels. I believe that one's basic mode of designation need not follow the mode of designation of one's previous life. For us, who are well trained in conventions, if we look at something blue, then the notion blue arises spontaneously. And for someone who is not yet trained in such conventions, the appearance will arise, and that will still imprint on the mind a generic idea that corresponds to it.

How an infant actually responds from its own side is probably unimaginable to us unless we have clairvoyance. The way it responds to events must, I believe, be influenced by its experiences in its previous life. If there were no force of familiarity from its previous life, then not even the desire for food, for example, would arise.

Chapter Three
How One Grasps onto True Existence

This presentation begins by establishing all phenomena as being conceptually designated, and then identifies the mode of grasping onto true existence, which is incompatible with the actual mode of existence of phenomena. The manner in which phenomena exist as conceptual designations has already been fairly extensively discussed.

To illustrate this, I gave the example of a hand, but you could equally take the body, or yourself. You too are merely a conceptual designation, but the meaning of this is a little easier to understand with respect to a hand. Still, when you actually meditate on emptiness, a major subject for analysis is the self. The reason for this is that the concepts of "I" and "mine" play a crucial role in our wandering about in the cycle of existence. To counter that, we must particularly focus on the lack of inherent existence of "I" and "mine."

The understanding of phenomena existing as conceptual designations can be equally applied to oneself, to others, and to all other phenomena. In terms of establishing emptiness, if one can establish this very effectively for one entity, one can see that it is equally applicable to all others. If one can clearly realize the lack of true existence of oneself—identify the manner of grasping onto true existence of oneself—and recognize that while one lacks true existence, one can nevertheless perform all human activities that are attributed to oneself, then with that understanding with regard to oneself, one can apply the same reasoning to all other entities.

In terms of the basis of designation of "I," one can, for example, speak of the mere collections of the five psycho-physical aggregates, or alternatively, one can speak of the mere assembly of the body and mind. Upon this basis we designate various things. We designate the basis of imputation of the "I"; we say this is this and that is that; we identify and label many parts and many attributes. When examining this array of components, it seems simply like a collection of things that can fall apart at any time. It is as if the many parts had been somehow forcibly held together. Thus, the actual mode of existence somehow seems inconceivable and inexpressible.

Inspect the manner in which you appear to yourself; inspect your own sense of "I." You may find that the self that appears to the mind is not a composite of a lot of things that came together. Rather, it seems to exist in and of itself. The actual mode of existence and the way we apprehend it (our own sense of this reality) are utterly incompatible. Isn't that so? The mind that apprehends the self in this way—a way that is utterly incompatible with reality—is called ignorance. However, it is clear that if one realizes the manner in which phenomena exist as mere conceptual designations, it is easy to understand how one grasps onto true existence. So how do we become deluded?

The answer is that at first we designate a certain object; we label it. In the early phases of labeling a certain entity we say, "This is called this, that is called that." We do not yet say, "This *is* this." During that phase, ignorance is not yet functioning. The entity appears as if it is truly existent, but it is not yet apprehended that way. This process is quite evident when we learn a new language. There is a phase when we have to remind ourselves, "This is called this," and "That is called that." During this time nothing has been reified yet. But then we become more habituated with the new language. After a while we no longer have the sense that we are imputing something on these entities. The phrase "This is called a flower" seems to be artificial, and we have the sense that it *is* a flower from its own side. We lose the sense of these things being merely designated; we lose the sense of their being what they are by the force of agreement, by the force of convention. They are reified with the sense that this is simply the way they are. The object that is so apprehended to exist in and of itself is regarded as truly existent, but in reality such a truly existent object does not exist at all. Although there is no true existence, without the realization of emptiness, we identify objects as truly existent.

When one is meditating on the emptiness of the self, one is meditating on the absence of an inherent self, or truly existent self; one is not meditating upon the nonexistence of the self that is designated. Following the realization of the absence of a truly existent self, of a truly existent "I," one establishes the self as being merely designated.

To repeat, in the first phase we impute a label or a designation on something, and then we forget that we have done so. Through that forgetting process an erroneous mental process takes place. The object itself appears in a mistaken way, and we grasp onto it. That mind that mistakenly grasps onto phenomena is called ignorance. Ignorance always entails reification. In this way we grasp onto the true existence of ourselves, and similarly, when focusing on an adversary, we grasp onto that person as truly existent. We also grasp onto loved ones as truly existent. This is how attachment and aversion arise automatically.

To reiterate: first there is the perception, and then we conceptually designate the object. The mere process of conceptually designating something basically means that we designate something as being present. But we do not designate all of its possible attributes. When we grasp onto the true existence of something, we grasp onto a presumed quality. This is where ignorance becomes involved, which leads to attachment and other mental afflictions.

Remember that the term "ignorance" (Tib. *ma rig pa*) literally means "not knowing," but this does not simply mean a lack of knowledge. In this context if we take "knowing" to be realizing emptiness, ignorance is not merely not realizing emptiness; rather, ignorance is so called because it stands in direct opposition to such knowing. As an analogy, a lie is not merely an untrue statement, rather it stands in direct opposition to a true statement. If we say that there is a hand here, then that phrase is a true phrase because it accords with reality. But if we say that there is no hand here, then that is a lie. This is so not only because it is not true, but because such a phrase is incompatible with the presence of the hand there. It stands in direct opposition to that truth.

TWO TYPES OF IGNORANCE

There are two types of ignorance, just as there are two types of mental afflictions (Tib. *nyon mongs*, Skt. *kleśa*). One is inborn, while the other is artificial. Inborn ignorance is instinctive, for it is something that all sentient beings are born with. It is a natural, inborn, instinctively false way of apprehending reality. For human beings it manifests clearly as this sense of "I am." Animals also have such ignorance, since they grasp onto themselves in a somewhat comparable way to the way human beings do. It is difficult to say exactly how their way of sensing their own identities differs from that of humans.

In contrast to inborn ignorance, there is artificial ignorance. Only those people who subject themselves to some form of intellectual training, or education, are prone to artificial ignorance. How does this occur? One learns things, thinks a lot, and speculates that things exist in such and such a way. There are many Buddhists and non-Buddhists who succumb to artificial ignorance. In fact, I suspect scientists quite possibly become heavily involved in artificial ignorance. Such people are actually trying to find out what is true, but not finding it, they settle on conjecture. This ignorance is called artificial.

In certain non-Buddhist philosophies, the "I" is posited as something that exists apart from the psycho-physical aggregates. One of the reasons for positing such a self is the belief that the "I" doesn't change at all. Don't you kind of feel that you are not subject to change? If you do, it shows that you have some strong habitual propensities for that sense of self-identity. That is a type of artificial ignorance that grasps onto the self; it is actually based on inborn ignorance. But the artificial ignorance even further reifies the self, grasping onto it all the more strongly. For example, you may think, "When I was a child, that was me, and nowadays, this is me, and when I get older, that will be me too." A sense of an "I" arises that persists without going through all the changes of the actual person.

Even if you realize the nonexistence of this enduring "I," this object of conjecture, even if you familiarize yourself with the realization of its nonexistence and are able to gain a perceptual realization of it, you do not necessarily become an *ārya*. Generally speaking, gaining a perceptual realization of emptiness, or subtle identitylessness, means that you become an *ārya*, a superior being. However, gaining a realization of the emptiness of this "I" that is grasped by artificial ignorance does not mean that you are an *ārya*, even if it is a perceptual realization. The point is that you need to utterly eradicate the mode of grasping of the inborn ignorance. You need to realize the utter nonexistence of the "I" that is grasped by the inborn ignorance. By the force of realizing the utter nonexistence of the "I" grasped by instinctive ignorance, all mental afflictions are attenuated. All artificial mental afflictions arise as a result of artificial ignorance, while all inborn mental afflictions are based upon the inborn ignorance.

It is said that the sense of touch pervades all the other sense faculties. This means that if one lacks the tactile faculty, then all the other faculties, visual and so forth, will vanish. For example, the tongue has the capacity to feel, which is the tactile faculty, but it also has a faculty of taste. Likewise, the eyes have both a tactile faculty and the visual faculty. While the visual faculty acts as the dominant condition for the perception of color and forms, the tactile faculty acts as the dominant condition for the awareness of tactile sensations.

If there were no reified sense of personal identity, no sense of "I" existing in and of itself, then all that would remain would be a lot of designated objects, so mental afflictions such as attachment and hostility could not arise. Isn't it true that as long as we grasp onto the self as something that exists in and of itself, this naturally leads to all the other mental afflictions? If we realized the manner in which we simply impute our own existence—if we realized how artificially this takes place—then by and large thoughts of craving one thing after another would not arise. Thus, it is important to realize the manner in which attachment and aggression are generated.

For example, when hostility for another person arises, one is implicitly grasping onto that person as being truly existent. Based upon that grasping, various hostile intentions arise. Grasping onto the true existence of various types of objects acts as the basis for seeing them as desirable, undesirable, or neutral. In contrast, if one can see the manner in which these things have been forcibly designated, then it is easy to see the deceptiveness of their mode of existence. But insofar as one sees the deceptiveness of them, then attachment and hostility are not likely to arise. It is like craving bubbles. One simply sees the superficial appearance of the bubble and does not crave it. So it is for all phenomena: they are all mere appearances, but then conceptualization sets in, designates, reifies, and we become entrenched in a myriad of mental afflictions.

The illusions of horses and elephants conjured up by a magician are mere apparitions. If we realize their apparitional nature, desire and hostility are not likely to arise toward them. In the absence of anything really—meaning truly, or inherently—being out there, we construe things as if there really were something there. Moreover, we may construe something as being frightful, so we get afraid, and then the ignorance and fear begin interacting. But it is all contrived. This is true of all knowable objects, of all entities. We simply agree: we establish the convention that some things are agreeable, and that some things are not agreeable, and we cycle around in pleasure and pain.

Take the example of gold and diamonds. The fact that these are very valuable is purely a matter of conventional agreement. If you place a chunk of gold and a diamond right next to an animal, it would not even make a hair of difference to the animal. It would just sit there. The fact that we do more than just sit there, thinking they are something very precious, comes by the force of our conventional agreement. It is said that *arhats*, beings who are liberated from the cycle of existence, make no such distinctions: their response to gold and a rock is exactly the same. They feel no desire for one or aversion to the other. They have no need for either. Cycling around in *saṃsāra* is not something that is done to us by something or someone else; rather, it is a process that is instigated and perpetuated by our own minds. However, when the confusion of the mind is dispelled, then even without anybody doing something to us, *nirvāṇa* is naturally attained.

Moreover, if one were able to realize the nature of the mind at all times as it is, one would be a *buddha*. A *tantra* states that one who fully realizes the nature of the mind is called a *buddha*. And a *sūtra* states that if one realizes the nature of the mind, one is a supreme *buddha*. Thus, one is encouraged not to look for spiritual awakening, or buddhahood, apart from one's own mind. *The Heart Sūtra* states, "Having fully passed beyond error, they have gone to the culmination of *nirvāṇa*." In short, a *buddha* is one who continually realizes the nature of one's own mind, and an unenlightened sentient being is one who does not.

If we want to understand how confusion operates in the mind, we can take the well-known example of mistaking a striped rope for a snake. In reality there is no snake; however, on the basis of asserting a snake, attachment to oneself arises, followed by the thought, "That snake will hurt me," followed by the intent to destroy the snake with a motivation of hostility. Similarly, within this body and mind there is ultimately no truly existent self; nevertheless, we assert the true existence of the self. Most of our activities are brought forth by mental afflictions. But by realizing the lack of true existence of the self, such afflictions as attachment and anger do not arise.

The strength of attachment and hostility also depends on the degree to which one regards the object as being related to oneself. For instance, if one is focusing upon a forest that belongs to oneself, this would give rise to stronger mental afflictions; one would be focusing on "my" forest. On the other hand, if one simply looks at a forest, one may regard it as pleasant, but attachment and avarice may not arise as strongly. Even if one is attending to objects that do not belong to oneself, there is no certainty that one's mental afflictions will be weak. For example, one may feel very strong attachment or hostility toward people who are in positions of great power.

THREE WAYS OF APPREHENDING AN OBJECT

There are three ways of apprehending an object: 1) apprehending it as being truly existent, 2) apprehending it as not truly existent, and 3) apprehending it without distinguishing between true existence or the lack of true existence. For a non-*ārya* who has nevertheless gained a realization of emptiness all of the above three will be operative. For a person who has not gained a realization of emptiness only the first and the last will be operative.

At the outset we may say "This is called a flower." However, as soon as we say, "This is a flower," we begin grasping onto the flower as if it were truly existent from the side of its basis of designation. We can ascertain this experientially. For instance, when you are introduced to a person, you may try to remember, "This person is called Tashi." When you meet the person for a second time you may wonder, "What is this person called?" It gets easier and easier, and after a while you say, "This *is* Tashi." Bear in mind that the basis of designation and the conceptual designation of the object are simultaneous. As soon as something is designated it exists.

When a person who is not philosophically inclined is in the process of labeling "This is a flower," such a person does not think, "This is a noninherently existent flower." This person does not make such a distinction, but simply labels it as a flower. An *arhat* or *ārya* who has gained a realization of emptiness says, "This is called a flower," while realizing that it is noninherently existent.

Many methods are used to realize emptiness. One may rely on the guidance of a spiritual mentor or on authentic scriptural sources. By listening to teachings and reflecting upon them at length, one gets to a point where one seems to penetrate to the meaning, and one feels some comfort there. One feels at ease, with one's own experience conforming to the teachings and treatises that one has relied upon. It is at this time that realization of emptiness occurs.

Before you gain realization of emptiness you need to establish the meaning of emptiness, and this must be done through discursive thought. As you meditate on it and realize it conceptually, then the realization gradually shifts from a conceptual to a nonconceptual state. It is said that by meditating with concepts the thoughts themselves extinguish conceptualization. This is like rubbing two pieces of wood together until they incinerate each other. There are two types of realizations: nonconceptual, direct realization and conceptual realization in which the generic idea still persists.

Three mental processes have to be understood in order to grasp what is meant by "realization." First, one may simply not fathom something; second, one may actively misunderstand it; and third, one may remain uncertain about it. Realization entails overcoming all those three mental processes. If one sees something, there is no certainty that one has realized it. Seeing is not necessarily realizing. For example, you can see a blue mountain, but you cannot realize, or genuinely apprehend, a blue mountain.

You may gain a realization of emptiness, and it may persist for a while, but then you slip back into your mental afflictions again. When the wisdom that realizes emptiness arises, that already somewhat counteracts the avenues for the mental afflictions. But you have to continue to draw energy into that wisdom and absorb your mind in it. You will then find that less and less of your practice will be tainted by mental afflictions. You will be able to bring your full awareness into wisdom, at which point the mental afflictions will no longer arise. This is like heating a pot of water. As you put the pot on the flame, the water does not suddenly come to a boil. Rather, it slowly gets warmer and warmer until the heat dominates it. When you turn the flame down, the cold gradually dominates. So it is with ignorance and all its derivative mental afflictions. This is why it is so important to cultivate attentional stability. By simply establishing attentional stability, many of the manifest mental afflictions are attenuated. But this does not mean that they no longer arise. Still, if one enhances the stability of mind with the realization of emptiness it is a very powerful tool.

The realization of emptiness really means to fathom how things are. If things existed by their own nature—existing in and of themselves—other phenomena would not be able to affect them in any way. In other words, if something is independent, or autonomous (Tib. *rang dbang*), it is not influenced by or dependent on anything else (Tib. *gzhan dbang*). But as soon as we assert that something exists independently of anything else, this implies it is not influenced by anything else. If something is independent there is nothing that can modify it. The contrary is also true: as soon as we posit something as being affected, modified, or influenced by other phenomena, there is no way to assert that it is independent; and that means it cannot be truly existent or autonomous.

For example, if we posit something as being absolutely long or short, it would have to be long or short without reference to anything else. It would have to be long or short by its own nature. Obviously, this is not the case. We can take our middle three fingers and say that the middle finger in relation to the ring finger is long, whereas the ring finger in relation to the middle finger is short. These are relational statements. The point of this discussion is that phenomena are devoid of independent existence. But this does not mean that they do not exist at all: they exist in a dependent fashion. They exist in relationship to and in reliance upon other phenomena.

THE IGNORANT VIEW CONCERNING A TRANSITORY ASSEMBLY

In his text *A Guide to the Middle Way* (*Madhyamakāvatāra*, I: 3) Candrakīrti comments that first there is clinging to the self, which is the type of ignorance that acts as the root of cyclic existence. The power of clinging to oneself as inherently existent leads to the clinging to that which is "mine." According to Prāsaṅgika Madhyamaka philosophy, this ignorance is called "the view concerning a transitory assembly" (Tib. *'jig tshogs la lta ba ma rig pa*). All mental afflictions and all suffering induced by the mental afflictions have as their source this mistaken view regarding a transitory assembly. It is the mind that clings to the self as truly, inherently existent; it is the mind that clings to the aggregates; and it is this mind that is called the view regarding the transitory assembly.

Grasping onto the true existence of other individuals is called ignorance, but that is not called the view regarding the transitory assembly. This view regarding the transitory assembly is said to be the principal cause for perpetuating one's continuing existence in the cycle of existence. This form of ignorance gives rise to desire and attachment. It attracts other mental afflictions like a magnet that attracts iron. Under the influence of ignorance and its resultant attachment sentient beings revolve in the cycle of existence, like water buckets on a water wheel. As soon as this form of ignorance is in action, our mental processes have no freedom, no will of their own, and no choice; they operate simply due to external circumstances.

Another classic analogy to illustrate the influence of desire and attachment is that of a deer drawn by the sweet music of a lute, who is then killed by a hunter's sling. In the same way, we are drawn by attachment and kept in the cycle of existence. Similarly, human beings' great attachment and clinging to reputation and fame becomes the source of suffering. Out of our desire and attachment for praise and good reputation, we strive arduously to attain these things, but in the process we find the result to be just the opposite of what we desired. In our attachment to wealth and food, we become like bees who get trapped and die in the honey in their hive, like moths who are attracted to a flame and perish in it, and like fish who go after bait and are hooked.

By means of these analogies, we can see how all of us are drawn inexorably by the power of desire and attachment. In this process we encounter different types of suffering, both the suffering of not meeting with what we desire and the suffering of meeting with what we don't desire. In short, attachment gives rise to a variety of problems, entailing both mental and physical suffering. In the absence of attachment one does not encounter that suffering. One can apply this to each of the analogies that were given. While experiencing attachment, one may have a certain sense of satisfaction or enjoyment, but eventually it gives rise to various types of suffering.

Candrakirti concludes the above verse by paying homage to the Buddha's great compassion for all sentient beings, but implicitly this also refers to the wisdom that realizes emptiness. Method and wisdom must always go together. In certain contexts the gradual stages of the path to spiritual awakening are explicit, while the wisdom of realizing emptiness is implicit. In other contexts the wisdom of realizing emptiness is explicitly discussed, while the stages of the path are implicit. All of this must be integrated. If one grasps onto the true existence of an object, this gives rise to attachment. However, if one does not grasp onto the true existence of an object, attachment will not be induced. For this reason one should counteract attachment with the wisdom that realizes emptiness.

Recall how we become deluded by grasping onto true existence. We start from a state of confusion. Then we label things; then we begin to identify the object with the label, until we become convinced that "This *is* this," or "This *is* me." This is a very important point, so it should not be forgotten. As long as there is simply the appearance of an object, and we give that appearance a label, there is no deception. However, due to our habituation to designations of phenomena, we fall into reification. If we fail to recognize this point, we will have a hard time understanding the distinction between the conventionally existent self and the self that is falsely grasped by ignorance.

The self that is grasped by ignorance should be refuted, but we should not refute the conventionally existent self. If we refute the self that is merely conventionally existent, that is like a seeing a person and saying, "Oh, I didn't see the person." Or we might look at another person and say, "All I see is the basis of designation of the person or the visual form of the body." This is no way to speak. It would be impossible to maintain any valid or justifiable use of language in this way. We would be negating the existence of a merely designated self, but we would not negate the self that is refuted by means of the wisdom that investigates the nature of emptiness. Once again, the self to be negated is the self which is grasped by ignorance.

In order to refute the existence of the self that is apprehended by ignorance, it is necessary to understand how ignorance grasps onto its object, namely, as being truly existent. Understanding the way that ignorance apprehends its object is to understand how phenomena are apprehended as being truly existent.

Chapter Four
The Four Essential Points

THE FIRST ESSENTIAL POINT

It is said that one establishes the view through a process that entails the four essential points. The first essential point is identifying the object to be refuted. As I mentioned earlier, in *A Guide to the Bodhisattva Way of Life* (IX: 139), Śāntideva states "Without detecting an imagined thing, its nonexistence is not apprehended," clearly indicating that one needs to refute the object apprehended by ignorance. One is not to refute that which is seen by the eyes, heard by the ears, or known by the mind. Then what is to be refuted? The true existence that is apprehended by ignorance, the ignorance that acts as the source of suffering.

As mentioned before, all the mental afflictions arise from the ignorant view regarding the transitory assembly, and the merely conventionally existent self is the attended object of such ignorance. Ignorance attends to the merely conventionally existent self, but apprehends it as a truly existent self, and it is that truly existent self which is to be refuted.

The Attended Object and the Attributed Object

At this point one needs to make a distinction between the attended object (Tib. *dmigs pa'i yul*) and the attributed object (Tib. *rnam pa'i yul*). The attended object is simply the "I," the conventionally existent "I," while the attributed object is the object apprehended as having a true existence falsely imputed upon it. It is the attributed "I," that truly existent "I," which is to be refuted.

When we encounter a person what we see is the aggregate of the body. Seeing the aggregate of the body we say, "This is such and such a person." In doing so, we conventionally designate the person upon the basis of the body. Not being satisfied with merely apprehending the conventionally existing person, we grasp onto the person as if he existed in and of himself. In this way grasping onto true existence takes place.

Isn't it true in terms of our own experience as we conceive of and apprehend ourselves and others? Don't we see individuals, these selves, as being real and solid? For example, when we think, "I am learned," or "I am in good health," or "I am clever," isn't it as if something were there that is the self, the "I"? In comparison with the merely conventionally existent self, the self that is apprehended as being truly existent seems quite firm, solid, and tangible. This is how ignorance apprehends things. The basis for this apprehension of the self as being truly existent is the merely conventionally existent self.

As I commented earlier, this process of conceptual designation entails focusing on the basis of designation and then forcefully imputing upon that a designated phenomenon. Having imputed that phenomenon upon a given basis of designation, there follows a sense of its being "out there." Therefore, to speak quite accurately, if one were asked, "Are you a human being?" the appropriate answer would be, "I am called a human being." Because the human being is not to be found under analysis, one should not say "I am a human being" with the sense that one is intrinsically a human being, independent of any conceptual designation.

The attended object is the object that is seen, and the mere seeing is the attending (Tib. *dmig pa*) to it. In dependence upon attending to the object, there arises the sense that it is truly existent. The "I," for instance, is thought to really exist in and of itself. So the attribute of true existence is applied to that being, and such an attribute is affirmed. With this affirmation there arises the attribute (Tib. *rnam pa*) of ignorance, and this truly existent "I" is the attributed object (Tib. *rnam pa'i yul*).

In your practice put to yourself the following questions: How am I looking at my object? Am I just attending to it, or am I attributing a quality to it? What do I see? Do I see simply the attended object, or do I see the object attributed with true existence? If you understand these distinctions, then you can apply them to all other types of conceptualizations or modes of understanding.

Here is the distinction between ignorance and the wisdom realizing emptiness: Ignorance attending to the basis of a merely conventionally existent self apprehends a truly existent self. Ignorance attends to the merely conventionally existent self, and that is its attended object. In contrast, the wisdom that realizes emptiness apprehends the absence of inherent existence. In other words, the attribute of the wisdom that realizes emptiness is its apprehension of the lack of inherent existence. Hence, the absence of inherent existence is the attributed object of the wisdom that realizes emptiness. That wisdom attends to the mere "I," which is conventionally existent, and that is its attended object. Therefore, both ignorance and the wisdom realizing emptiness have the same attended object, and they attend to the same thing, but the attributes of those two mental processes and their attributed objects are mutually incompatible. Regarding the attended object, the wisdom realizing emptiness refutes the attributed object grasped by ignorance.

On the one hand, we may have a cognitive apprehension of the conventional or relative "I," which is not the same as the wisdom realizing emptiness, and on the other hand we have the apprehension of the "I" by ignorance. However, the attentional processes for these two are very different. The attended object of the mind that apprehends the conventional self, and the attended object of ignorance, the reified "I," are different. Why is this so? The attended object of the mind that grasps the relative "I" is the basis of designation of the "I," namely the aggregates. In contrast, the attended object of ignorance is the self. Now the "I" and the basis of designation upon which the "I" is designated are mutually exclusive; one is never the other.

To take another example, the attended object of great compassion is all sentient beings. The attribute of great compassion is the yearning "May I free all sentient beings from suffering." Similarly, in the case of great loving-kindness, the attended object is all sentient beings, and the attribute of that mental state is the yearning "May I bring all sentient beings to joy."

Bear in mind that ignorance as defined here is a conceptual state of mind. One can speak of a basis of observing phenomena, and also of a basis of conceiving, or apprehending, phenomena. This twofold distinction in the mode of observation and the mode of apprehension holds true for all forms of conceptualization. For sensory perception, which of course is nonconceptual, there is no distinction between the mode of observation and the mode of apprehension. For instance, in the visual perception of a flower the attended object and the attributed object are one and the same. We may see a white flower and a red flower, which are the attended objects, and their red or white attributes are different than the flowers themselves. So clearly, attributes include many qualities other than the attribute of true existence.

In contrast, in the context of conceptualization the term "attribute" (Tib. *rnam pa*) refers to the aspect of conceptual grasping in which one identifies one thing as opposed to another. For example, if one thinks, "This is a flower," in that process the conceptual mind apprehends the flower and that very apprehension is the attribute of that mind. In the case of attending to the basis of designation of a flower, the attended object is the basis of designation, and what is apprehended is the flower, which becomes the attributed object.

It is important to be clear about the difference between a basis of designation and a designated object. At times the attended object arises as the basis of designation, and at other times it will be the designated object. Similarly, the attributed object may on some occasions be the basis of designation, and on other occasions it may be the designated object. For the mind that apprehends the mere self, the conventionally existent self, the attended object is the basis of designation of the "I." For the mind that apprehends the basis of designation of the "I," the aggregates which are the basis of designation also become the attributed object.

The designated object may also be the attended object. For example, the self as a designated object is the attended object of both the ignorance that apprehends the self, as well as that of the wisdom that realizes the lack of inherent existence of the self. The mind that thinks, "I am," simply grasps the conventionally existent self, and for that mind, the self is also the attributed object. For the mind that apprehends the basis of designation, that very basis of designation serves as the attributed object. For the cognition that apprehends the designated object, the designated object serves as the attended object for that mind. As you are observing a flower, if you attend to the basis of designation of the flower and you think, "This is the basis of designation," then this basis of designation is the attributed object. But for the mind that thinks, "This is a flower," the basis of designation is now the attended object, while the flower itself is the attributed object. For the deluded mind that apprehends the flower as being truly existent, the conventionally existent flower is the attended object, while the truly existent flower is the attributed object.

On the basis of appearances we can speak of and conceive of the basis of designation, and we can speak of and conceive of a designated object. But we need to see the distinction between the basis of designation and the designated object. For example, with reference to the person, the psycho-physical aggregates are the basis of designation, and the "I" is the designated object. Consider the phrases, "I am truly existent," "I am inherently existent," "I exist by my own characteristics," "I exist by my own nature," "I exist purely objectively," and "I exist as a self." All these statements are synonymous. Moreover, such phrases as "absence of true existence," "not existing by one's own nature," "not existing from one's own side," "not existing inherently," "not existing objectively," and "not existing as an identity," are all synonymous too. At times ignorance is called "grasping onto the self" (Tib. *bdag 'dzin*), and sometimes it is referred to as "grasping onto true existence" (Tib. *bden 'dzin*). These terms are used interchangeably, so don't be confused!

Now let's turn to the following question: Is the conventional existence of an object such as a flower independent of anybody actually observing it? When one speaks of a certain object being established, this means that it appears to the mind. It does not depend on anything else. If something does not appear to the mind, the issue of whether or not it exists cannot even be raised. Therefore, it is said that an object and the awareness of that object are mutually interdependent. In other words, if there is awareness, there must be an object of awareness, and if there is an object of awareness there must be awareness. If one of those two is missing then the other cannot possibly be established.

The mere fact that something is conceptually designated does not necessarily indicate that it exists. If it did, then blue snow-mountains could exist, for these appear to people with a certain eye disorder. In other words, if all it took for something to exist is that it is conceptually designated, then anything that comes to mind would exist. Moreover, although there is a designation of the self as being truly existent, it does not follow that this independent, permanent self in fact does exist. Even though it may be conceptually designated, that does not imply that it exists. The same is true of a Creator. Although a Creator is conceived and conceptually designated, it does not necessarily follow that such a being exists. Even in Buddhist treatises there are references to a creator of the universe. For example, in *A Guide to the Middle Way* Candrakīrti states that the mind creates the universe, and *A Treasury of Knowledge* (*Abhidharmakośa*) states that the manifold worlds arise from *karma*. Still, these theories are very different from a theistic system, and the point is that a Creator does not necessarily exist in the way it is conceived. Just because something is conceived and designated does not mean that it exists.

Conventional and Ultimate Analysis

I have explained the distinction between the attended object and the attributed object, pointing out that it is the attributed object of ignorance that is to be refuted. True existence enters in as the attributed object. When one is satisfied with the mere conventional existence of a given object, this is deemed a conventional mode of apprehending that object. If one establishes an object merely as something nominally established by its label, this is the conventional mode of establishing the existence of the phenomenon. It is the conventional mode of analysis. For example, one may ask, "What is this?" and another person may respond, "This is a flower." If we respond, "Oh, I see, this is a flower," without asking why is this a flower or what makes this a flower, then that is the conventional establishment of this phenomenon. It does not entail an investigation into the ultimate mode of existence of the flower.

In terms of conventional analysis, in contrast to ultimate analysis, there are indeed reasons why one posits something as being what it is. This does not mean that it is simply taken on authority. An example would be if I say, "I need to go," and someone asks, "Why do you need to go?" and I reply, "Because it is time for me to go to work." This is conventional reasoning. This is the type of reasoning one accepts while being satisfied with the mere conceptual designation. Similarly, when somebody says, "There is a fire over there," someone else may ask, "How do you know?" The first person may answer, "Well, there is smoke." The person is reasoning that wherever there is smoke there has to be a fire. This, too, is conventional reasoning.

This conventional mode of analysis does not lead to the realization of emptiness. So what mode of analysis does lead to a realization of emptiness?

Take the statement, "This is a flower." One may not be satisfied with the mere conventional designation, "This is a flower," but may instead proceed to ask, "What exactly is there that is a flower? Is it the stem, is it the petals, is it the roots, the left side, the right side?" Probing in this way constitutes ultimate analysis. To relate this to the self, one begins by saying, "This is 'I.'" If one justifies this by saying, "This person here is called 'I,'" that is simply conventional analysis. But one who is not satisfied with the mere conceptual designation, "This is 'I,'" will instead proceed to ask, "What exactly here is the 'I'? Is the body this 'I'? Is the mind this 'I'?" In this way one goes beyond conventional reasoning.

Why should one engage in this second type of analysis? The reason for this is because ignorance apprehends its object as if it exists purely objectively. In other words, ignorance apprehends its object as if it exists entirely from its own side. If phenomena in fact existed in this way—purely objectively from their own side—then the more carefully one investigated them, the more clearly those objects would appear to the mind. However, the more closely one examines phenomena, the more one sees that objects are not to be found under such analysis. That is why one should not remain satisfied with mere conventional analysis or reasoning.

Let's draw an analogy. If a certain situation is true, then the more carefully we examine the situation, the more clearly it appears to be true. Let's say there are two people in a dispute and we examine their claims very carefully. If one of them is telling the truth and the other is lying, then the more carefully we examine the evidence, the more clearly the truth will appear as the truth. The same holds true for false claims. Even though they may appear true in the beginning, when we inspect them closely, any kind of validity of the false claim disappears altogether.

When we use the word "attribute" (Tib. *rnam pa*), as in the attribute of ignorance or the attribute of the wisdom that realizes emptiness, then the attribute of ignorance is the very thought, "I am truly existent." The attributed object of ignorance is the true existence that is grasped by ignorance. And what is the attended object? It is the mere self. And what is the nature of the attention? It is the simple observation of the self. What is the attribute of the wisdom that realizes emptiness? It is the mind that understands that the "I" is not truly existent. And what is the attended object of the wisdom that realizes emptiness? It is simply the "I." And what is the nature of that attention? It is the very observation of the "I."

The attended object of the wisdom that realizes emptiness is called the basis of characteristics (Tib. *khyad gzhi*). It is this basis that has certain characteristics. Now the emptiness of the self, for example, is a characteristic of the self. The self is the basis of certain characteristics, and emptiness of the self is a such a characteristic. The cognition of the characteristic is called the attribute of that cognition, while the cognition of the basis of characteristics is called attention (Tib. *dmigs pa*).

THE SECOND ESSENTIAL POINT

The first of the four essential points is recognizing the object to be refuted. The second essential point is that this truly existent self is not identical with the aggregates, and the third essential point is that it is not distinct from the aggregates.

As I have stated, ignorance apprehends the "I" as being truly existent; it apprehends true existence with reference to the "I," and the "I" is apprehended upon its basis of designation, the psycho-physical aggregates. If I do in fact truly exist, then I would have to be truly existent among those aggregates. If a truly existent self could be found in the aggregates, then one or more of those aggregates should be this truly existent self. As we consider this possibility, we can ask, "Is the body the self? Is the mind the self?" We can follow an analysis along these lines. Taking on the one hand this truly existent "I," and on the other hand the aggregates, we can ask whether this truly existent self is identical with the aggregates or whether it is distinct from the aggregates.

Focusing on the second essential point let's ask, "Is this truly existent 'I' in fact identical with the aggregates?" If we accept this as a hypothesis, we should consider the fact that the aggregates are plural; in other words, there are many aggregates. For simplicity's sake, since one can speak of there being just two aggregates, namely the body and mind, and if both of these are posited as being identical to the "I," there should be two "I's." Alternatively, if we refer to the five aggregates, then each of the five aggregates should be identical with the "I," so there should be five selves. This consequence is problematic because in fact, there are not five selves; there is only one "I" per person.

Alternatively, one might argue that since there is but one "I" that is identical with the aggregates, it would follow that the five aggregates should be one entity. However, if that were the case, the very designation of "I" would become superfluous. Why? Because it would illuminate nothing; it would simply be one more name for the aggregates. No reference to the "I" as something distinct from the aggregates would be necessary. In short, there would be no need for the appellation of the word "I."

Let's briefly review the nature of these five aggregates.

• First, there is the aggregate of form, and this includes all the five sensory objects of form, sound, taste, smell, and touch, as well as the four elements of earth, water, fire, and air, which are respectively solidity, fluidity, heat, and motility.

• The second is the aggregate of feeling, which is an aspect of awareness. The aggregate of feeling includes feelings of pleasure, pain, and indifference.

• The third is the aggregate of recognition, the faculty of the mind that allows us to distinguish one thing or event from another. It is sometimes called discernment.

• The fourth is the aggregate of consciousness. This includes mental consciousness as well as the various types of sensory consciousness.

• The fifth aggregate is the aggregate of compositional factors. Once you have accounted for the aggregates of form, feeling, recognition, and consciousness, a lot of other factors remain, and they are all included in this fifth aggregate. This aggregate is normally listed as the fourth of the five aggregates, and it includes all the other factors of a person that are not included in the other four aggregates.

Clearly, these five aggregates are not one single thing. Recognizing this leads to the further recognition that the hypothetical truly existent self is not identical with the aggregates.

As an alternative hypothesis, we may consider the possibility that this postulated, truly existent "I" is identical not with all of the aggregates, but is just one among them. However, each of the aggregates is itself composed of many factors and components that must be taken into consideration. Thus, even if this truly existent "I" were identical with just one of the aggregates, the self would still be composed of a multitude of components. This single truly existent self would still have to become plural; it would have to become many things, for it would have to be identical with all the components of that one aggregate.

The conclusion we draw from these various hypotheses is that the hypothetical truly existent "I" is not identical with the aggregates, because the aggregates are many and the "I" is but one. The original hypothesis that the "I" is identical with the aggregates cannot be validated. Recognizing this leads to the certainty of the second essential point that the self is not identical with the aggregates.

THE THIRD ESSENTIAL POINT

As we turn to the third essential point, we ask whether this hypothetical truly existent "I" exists as something distinct from the aggregates. If it were, it would have to be utterly unrelated to them. Thus, once you have analytically set aside the body on one side and the mind on the other, there should be something left over that we could point to as the truly existent self. But no such self is to be found.

If one posits that the truly existent self may be the *collection* of all the aggregates, one should consider that there is no such collection apart from the body and mind. Rather, the collection of body and mind is designated upon the basis of body and mind. Therefore, we would say that the collection is not the truly existent "I." If the collection of body and mind were truly existent, then we should be able to find it under analysis. In other words, if we equate a truly existent "I" with the collection of the body and mind, then that collection must be truly existent. But if a truly existent collection of body and mind were the "I," then the "I" would have to be immutable. However, since the collection of the body and mind exists in dependence upon its components, it is constantly subject to change. So the truly existent "I" cannot be the collection of the body and mind, nor can it be distinct from that collection.

Now one may think that the realization of impermanence refutes the existence of the truly existent self, but this is not quite true. A realization of impermanence merely means that one realizes that as soon as something comes into existence it is impermanent and is in the process of deterioration. But the mind that realizes impermanence alone does not realize the lack of true existence. In fact, to an ordinary person who realizes impermanence, impermanence itself appears to be truly existent.

Generally speaking the "I" and the aggregates are established as being distinct from one another, since the aggregates belong to the "I." We therefore need to understand how this point shows the fallacy of the hypothesis of a truly existent self. To reiterate, we say "my aggregates," and this phrase clearly indicates that the person who has the aggregates is distinct from the aggregates. Here, the "I" and the aggregates are different, but we have already established that a truly existent "I" and the aggregates are not distinct. So where does the fault lie? The fault lies in postulating a truly existent self as being distinct from the aggregates. A truly existent "I" would have to be something that in no way depends upon the aggregates. Since there is no truly existent self that exists distinct from the aggregates and independent of them, this postulated truly existent self does not exist apart from the aggregates.

How then does the "I" exist? Here we are speaking not of a truly existent "I," but of the conventional "I." The "I" exists as something different from, but in dependence upon, the aggregates. Realizing that there is no self to be found under ultimate analysis leads to the certainty that this hypothetical truly existent self does not exist as distinct from the aggregates. This is the third essential point.

Valid and Invalid Ways of Postulating the Self

I would now like to review a major point, namely that the truly existent "I" is grasped on the basis of the conventional "I." The conventional "I" is apprehended on the basis of the aggregates and therefore, if we assume that the truly existent "I" does in fact exist, we can posit that it is in fact the aggregates. Having adopted that hypothesis, we can examine the consequences of that position and see how those consequences undermine the initial premise. Alternatively, if there is a truly existent "I" and it is not identical with the aggregates, it must be distinct from the aggregates. When we again examine the consequences from this premise, we identify all the aggregates, set them aside analytically, and then seek out the "I," but no such "I" is to be found. Here is the essential point: Conventionally speaking, the "I" is distinct from the aggregates, but no truly existent "I" can be established as distinct from the aggregates.

Let's now consider the notion of the self as a stream of consciousness by first investigating whether or not a stream of consciousness truly exists. In this regard, we may posit "true existence" in two ways: true existence in dependence upon other phenomena, and true existence that is independent of other phenomena. Ignorance apprehends the self as being truly existent, as something that is independent of anything else. This is how ignorance apprehends true existence. But there is another way of speaking of true existence, and that is by determining whether or not something is *conventionally* true. Speaking in this fashion does not imply that the object under investigation exists independently of anything else. For example, we may ask whether a person who appears on the television screen is a true person. The answer is no; it is not a true person. Next we can go on to ask whether this appearance of a person is truly an appearance of a person on the television screen. And here the answer is yes; the appearance is true. There truly is an appearance of a person on the television. Similarly, while looking in a mirror, I may look at the reflection of my face in the mirror and ask, "Is that my face?" The answer is "No, this is not my face." If this were truly my face, then it would have to have flesh and bones and so forth, but the image of the face in the mirror does not have those components. The reflection in the mirror is false in terms of being a face; even though it appears to be a face, in fact it is not one. But it truly is a reflection of a face. Just as the face in the mirror is not truly a face, so also is the true existence that is apprehended by ignorance untrue.

Now we may ask, "Are there then no true phenomena?" The answer is, of course, that there are many true phenomena. There is the true Buddha, the true Dharma, the true Saṅgha, and many other things that are true also. So now let's examine the suggestion that the continuum of consciousness is truly existent. What is meant by "continuum"? The term "continuum" is designated upon many sequential components. It has components and attributes, and they are all subject to change. But apart from those changing components and events, one cannot posit the existence of a continuum. So we must ask if this stream of consciousness is truly existent in the manner in which ignorance apprehends phenomena as being truly existent. The answer is no, it is not. Once again, consider what is meant by a continuum: it is something designated upon many components. Apart from the many components that make up the continuum, there is no way to judge that something *is* a continuum. Since by definition a continuum is something designated upon many parts, for that very reason the continuum must be deemed false in the sense of not being truly existent.

To illustrate the fact that consciousness is dependent upon the body, we can use the very fact that the variations of clarity of consciousness are dependent on such influences as our diet, our health, and so forth. As one fluctuates, so does the other fluctuate. There are certain physical causes for the degree of clarity of consciousness, so this already suggests that consciousness is not truly existent in the manner described previously. Furthermore, the very fact that one's consciousness yesterday may have been unclear whereas today it may be clear also suggests that consciousness is not truly existent. Unclear consciousness is surely influenced by other causal factors. Moreover, as unclear consciousness comes under the influence of other causal factors, it may transform into clear consciousness. Therefore, the hypothesis that this continuum of consciousness is truly existent in the sense that it is immutable is refuted.

Even the *buddha*-nature is something that is conceptually designated. Emptiness, too, is something that is conceptually designated. The mutual dependence between awareness and the object of awareness relates to the *buddha*-nature as well. If there is mutual interdependence in general between the object of awareness and the awareness, then more specifically the awareness that establishes *buddha*-nature and the *buddha*-nature which is the object of that awareness must also be mutually interdependent. In the absence of one, the other cannot be present. So anything that comes into existence through the power of being conceptually designated does not inherently exist; it does not truly exist. If there were something that did exist but was not conceptually designated, that would be truly existent. The process of conceptual designation is something quite forceful; there is nothing there from the object's own side, but things are forcefully imputed upon it conceptually. Thus, since the object is dependent on that designation, it does not truly exist.

In the Dzogchen, or Great Perfection, tradition, there are statements suggesting that what is called innate mind (Tib. *nyug sems*), or awareness (Tib. *rig pa*), is truly existent. Here the innate mind is said to be truly existent in the sense that it does not undergo fluctuations or changes, as do thoughts and conceptual states of mind. But the very term "awareness" is something that can be designated in relationship to its opposite:

nonawareness (Tib. *ma rig pa*), or ignorance. Because awareness is established in relationship to its opposite, it cannot therefore be truly existent in the Madhyamaka sense of the term. Moreover, the innate mind is posited in contrast to fluctuating states of mind, so this term is also designated in relationship to something else. Therefore, it too cannot be truly existent.

Single and Multiple Phenomena

Whatever phenomenon exists must be established as being either a single phenomenon or multiple phenomena. There is no third option. To give an example, one can ask whether a hand is present. The answer is yes, the hand is present. Then we can ask whether it is one thing or many things. Of course, we would respond that the hand is one thing. Nobody looks at a single hand and says, "There are many hands." And then, as we are establishing the fingers, we can ask whether they are one or many. Of course, they are established as many, because there is more than one finger on a hand.

Now let's take another illustration, that of a finger and the impermanence of a finger. These two phenomena are of the same nature. Regarding a finger, one can ask whether the finger and the impermanence of the finger are established as being one or many. As we visually observe a finger, we only see one phenomenon, the finger. But the conceptual mind can distinctly apprehend first, the finger, and second, the impermanence of the finger. To the conceptual mind they appear as distinct; they appear as multiple. For that reason the finger and the impermanence of the finger are established as plural, not as a unity.

Then we can ask whether conventional truth and ultimate truth are established as one or multiple. The answer is that they are established as distinct, as multiple. Again, there is no third option. That is, something may be unitary or it may be multiple. There is no third option of something that is neither a single entity nor a multiple entity. Any possible candidate between the two would fall into the category of being a multiple entity.

THE FOURTH ESSENTIAL POINT

This brings us to the fourth essential point, namely that an inherently existent entity, such as a truly existent "I," does not exist either as a single phenomenon nor as a multiple phenomenon. It does not exist at all, in any way whatsoever. This is called the essential point of inclusiveness. It is an all-inclusive principle: since it is neither single nor plural, it does not exist. By seeking out a truly existent phenomenon by means of the four essential points, such true existence as a single or multiple entity is not found, so it is therefore refuted. Through this mode of logical analysis, one consequence follows upon another, and the result is the refutation of true existence. It is at this very moment, as one arrives at the certain conclusion that this truly existent phenomenon does not exist either as a single entity or as multiple entities and therefore does not exist at all, that one is led to a realization of emptiness.

As a result of this analysis there comes a flash of insight that the self does not truly exist. It is very sharp, but fleeting. Subsequently, other thoughts come in and the insight is defused; it is lost. This is how it is at the beginning of such practice. However, as one becomes more and more accustomed to the practice, coming back to it again and again, the duration of the insight becomes longer and longer.

Simple and Complex Negations

The mind that realizes that there is no truly existent self is said to bear the attribute of a simple negation (Tib. *med dgag*). A simple negation is just a negation, without suggesting or implying the affirmation of any other phenomena. This can perhaps best be understood in terms of the example, "The *brahmin* does not drink alcohol." This statement simply negates an alcohol-drinking *brahmin*. Beyond that negation it does not suggest the affirmation of any other phenomenon. It does not suggest that the *brahmin* drinks something else. But let's look at a second statement: "The *brahmin* does not drink alcohol, but lives without thirst." What does this indicate? Clearly it suggests explicitly that the Brahman lives without thirst, but it implies that the *brahmin* drinks something else. The first example is a simple negation, while the second is a complex negation (Tib. *ma yin dgag*).

Returning to our discussion of the self, the statement that a truly existent self grasped by ignorance does not exist is a simple negation. It does not suggest the affirmation of any other phenomena. On the other hand, if one experiences or thinks that the truly existent self apprehended by ignorance does not exist, but in addition one has a sense of emptiness, then that experience is one of a complex negation.

These two statements are alike in that both are simple negations: "The *brahmin* does not drink alcohol," and "The self apprehended by ignorance does not exist." Both of these statements or thoughts negate a certain phenomenon without implying or suggesting the presence of another phenomenon. Similarly there is a parallel between these two phrases: "The *brahmin* does not drink alcohol, but he lives without thirst," and "The self apprehended by ignorance does not exist, but there is a sense of emptiness." Each of these statements not only negates something, but also suggests the presence of something else. If one affirms something beyond the simple negation, one is engaging in a complex negation.

Review of the Meditation on Emptiness
When you meditate on emptiness, you should do so on the basis of these four essential points. The first step of this meditative procedure is to examine carefully your own sense of "I" and the manner in which your own sense of "I," or personal identity, arises to the mind: "How do I seem to exist to myself?" You need to check it out for yourself. What comes to mind when you think of yourself? Does anything appear at all? Bring to mind the thought "I" and see what arises to the mind in terms of the mode of appearance of yourself. What would happen if someone said "You scoundrel"? Do you have a sense of "I" that arises in response to that? And what happens if someone comes and says, "You are a marvelous person"? Do you experience a sense of "I" in response to that?

Doesn't there arise a very tangible, firm sense of "I am"? Try to observe very carefully the manner in which your "I" appears on such occasions. If it appears as something quite tangible, it seems truly existent. Moreover, ignorance goes on to conceptually grasp it and apprehend it as being truly existent.

As you bear in mind this mode of appearance and this mode of apprehension of this truly existent "I," with one facet of your awareness you should vividly hold in mind these modes of appearance and apprehension, and with another facet of your mind you should examine the object that appears and is apprehended in that way.

This truly existent "I" that is so apprehended is grasped on the basis of the self, the "I," which, in turn, is apprehended on the basis of the body and/or mind. If it is apprehended on the basis of the body, you should ask, "Is this truly existent 'I' the body?" But you find that it is not because we say, "This is 'my' body." Since the "I" possesses the body, it is not the same as the body. If the body is not the truly existent self, or "I," then we can ask if the mind is the "I." But once again we say "my" mind. Since, like the body, the mind is an object that belongs to the "I," they are distinct. Thus, the mind cannot be that truly existent "I." This is another proof for the second essential point, namely that the truly existent "I" is not identical to the aggregates. This second essential point is that the truly existent self and the aggregates are not identical.

Having ascertained that the truly existent self is not identical to the aggregates, you may wonder if the "I" exists apart from the body and mind. But again, if you analytically set the body and mind aside, then no truly existent self apart from those is to be found. For example, if I take myself as an example, I can set aside my body, and then I can set aside my mind, but then, is there anything left to be recognized apart from these two? Clearly there is nothing.

As a result of such analysis a certainty arises that there is no such "I," and you abide in that ascertainment. When you reach such a point in your meditative practice, dwell for a while in that recognition, in the realization that there is not such an "I." Dwell in it for a while, then return to the analysis once again, and lead yourself again to that certainty. Then abide in the certainty, but as it becomes diffuse, go back to the analysis. Continue in this way, practicing in an alternating fashion.

It is relatively easy to ascertain that the body is not the truly existent self, nor is the mind the truly existent self. By engaging in this type of analysis, slowly one recognizes that the truly existent self apprehended by ignorance does not exist. If one were to affirm the existence of the self apprehended by ignorance, it would lead to the false consequences described earlier. In this way one realizes the nonexistence of that self. However, you should recognize that this analysis does not give a stable, single-pointed realization. It can lapse and become diffuse.

To repeat a crucial point, the truly existent self apprehended by ignorance is apprehended with reference to the self, and the self is apprehended with reference to the aggregates. You can pose to yourself the hypothesis that if the "I" is truly existent, then it must exist on the basis of the aggregates. If the truly existent "I" is present among the aggregates, then those aggregates must be the truly existent self. But which aggregate? One can speak of five aggregates, or for simplicity's sake, one can simply speak of the body and mind. In terms of the body and mind, which one of these is identical to the "I"?

Looking at the first alternative, that the body is identical to the self, we can point out that the body has five appendages: the two legs, two arms, and the neck and head. Are any of those five appendages the "I"? If we say that the head is the "I," then we can analyze further and note that the head itself is not simply one entity, but rather is a composite of many attributes: the ears, the eyes, and so forth. Now which of these is the self? Of course, the self is none of these things. To ignorance the "I" appears as something very tangible and substantial. But if the "I" were really present within the aggregates, then by means of such an analysis we would find this very tangible, substantial self.

Let's take an analogy. If you were to look for your father within a specific group of people, you bring to your search a certain image of what your father looks like. As you examine every person in the group, you are looking for a fit: you would think, "Is there a person here who corresponds to the image I have in mind?" When you find someone in this group of people whose appearance corresponds to the image you have in mind, then you think, "Ah, this is my father." However, if you have examined everyone in the room, but have not found anyone whose face is a replica of the image that you have in mind, then you think, "My father is not here."

Similarly, ignorance projects a certain image of a truly existent self, like the image you have of your father. So you investigate the body and the mind to see whether anything within the body and mind corresponds to this image of a truly existent self. But when you examine the body and its various components, looking for something corresponding to this image, you do not find anything. By examining the body and mind you come to the conclusion that there is no truly existent self. That very ascertainment is the ascertainment of emptiness.

Please do not forget this sequential relationship: the truly existent "I" is apprehended on the basis of the conventional "I," and the conventional "I," or simply the self, is apprehended on the basis of the aggregates. Therefore, if the truly existent "I" is to exist, it must be present among those aggregates. This is a crucial point that is not articulated clearly in Madhyamaka treatises on emptiness.

Another important point that is not usually expressed clearly in Madhyamaka treatises is the procedure of recognizing the image, or the sense, of the self as it is apprehended by ignorance, and trying to find something corresponding to that. This vital point is the stumbling block for Yogācārins and for Svātantrika Mādhyamikas, which they fail to understand. Contemplatives following these other philosophical systems come to the conclusion that the self is not to be found, but since there has to be something that goes from one lifetime to another, it must be the mind. They therefore assert that the mind is the self. Others assert that the collection of the aggregates is the "I," or that the continuum of the aggregates is the "I." On the one hand such contemplatives don't find the self, but on the other hand they affirm that there must be someone who takes rebirth; there must be someone who engages in actions; there must be someone who experiences the karmic law of cause and effect. For that to be true, they believe, there must be some basis in reality for this self. The Svātantrika Mādhyamikas, for example, call mental consciousness the "I," because they say it is this consciousness that takes rebirth.

Our analysis leads to the ascertainment that this truly existent "I" that is apprehended by ignorance does not exist. As a result of this analysis one examines whether or not something corresponding to this *sense* of a truly existent "I" objectively exists, but nothing is objectively found. Nevertheless, this image, or sense, of a truly existent self is present in the mind. To the mind that realizes emptiness by way of an idea, the basis that has been analyzed still appears, and it has the attribute of being empty. In Tsongkhapa's own writings, he states that the attribute of emptiness appears to the mind that realizes emptiness by way of an idea. Nevertheless, the textbooks of the three major Gelugpa monastic universities [Sera, Drepung, and Ganden] all seem to refute Tsongkhapa on this point by saying that the self does not appear to the mind that realizes emptiness by way of an idea. The reason they give is that since emptiness is a simple negation, the basis of emptiness does not appear to the mind that realizes emptiness. In fact, however, one realizes this simple negation on the basis of the aggregates and not on the basis of the self. To repeat, the truly existent self is apprehended with reference to the self, and the self is apprehended with reference to the aggregates. In other words, if the truly existent self were to exist, it would have to exist among the aggregates, and therefore one would have to be the aggregates. One is then forced to realize the absence of a truly existent self with reference to the aggregates. One is not trying to find out whether or not the self exists at all. It seems that these textbook writers did not consider this matter in sufficient depth. Tsongkhapa stated very clearly that the basis of emptiness does appear to that mind, and there is no contradiction in asserting that both the basis of emptiness and emptiness itself appear to one mind.

When realizing emptiness by way of an idea, this means that on the one hand you realize emptiness—emptiness appears to your mind—but together with that and merged inextricably with emptiness itself is an idea of emptiness. It is called a generic idea (Tib. *don spyi*). So there are two things that appear to the mind: both emptiness and an idea of emptiness. When seeking out the designated entity (Tib. *btags don*), the truly existent self is not found.

In the aforementioned analogy, the image of your father appears in your mind, and then you look for something corresponding to that image in order to find your father. Similarly, as you bear in mind some idea of a truly existent self, you seek something corresponding to that idea in the aggregates, but you do not find it. This leads to the certainty that such a self corresponding to that image does not exist. But it does not lead to the conclusion that there is no self whatsoever.

Realizing this, you can further ponder, "How is it that I accumulate the habitual propensities from actions and experience the results of actions? How do I exist?" The answer is, "I exist as something simply designated. I exist by conventional agreement." Tsongkhapa takes this position: There is a self that accumulates habitual propensities from actions and experiences the results from actions. There is no doubt about this. However, since the self does not exist objectively from its own side, there is no alternative but to conclude that the self exists purely by conceptual designation. Therefore, it is clear that the self exists in dependence upon other things. In the Prāsaṅgika Madhyamaka system, this means that the self is dependent upon conceptual designation. There is a mutual interdependence between the designator and the designated object. Nothing can be designated without a designator. As I commented earlier, in the absence of a designator it is impossible to establish the existence of anything whatsoever.

Generally speaking, the basis of designation of the "I" and the "I" come into being simultaneously. To give a specific example, if upon the basis of a certain aggregate we designate a person as Tashi, then Tashi's basis of designation (the aggregate) and Tashi himself come into being simultaneously. Before this designation is made, one can ask whether there is anything there. Is there a body or a child that is about to be called Tashi? The answer is yes. But the body or the aggregates do not become the basis of designation of Tashi until that designation is made.

The very terms "inconceivable" and "inexpressible" are themselves conceptual designations. If it were possible to find and to identify some phenomenon without naming it, then that phenomenon would exist independently of conceptual designation. But as soon as we identify something by naming it, there is no alternative but to assert that it is something that is conceptually designated. Even the very notion of existence is conceptually designated. The idea that "this exists" is a conceptual designation. The very category of existence is something conceptually designated. It then goes without saying that in the specific instance of something that is existent, that is also conceptually designated.

Bear in mind that even the basis of designation itself is conceptually designated. Moreover, as soon as you speak of a basis of designation, this already implies the presence of a designated object. The two, the basis of designation and the designated object that is imputed upon that basis, come into being simultaneously, and they are of the same nature. But do not confuse this statement with the false assertion that the basis of designation and the object designated upon that basis are one and the same thing. They are not. The basis of designation depends for its existence upon the designated object, and the designated object depends for its existence upon the basis of designation. Furthermore, both of those are dependent upon the designating mind. Should you ask whether there is any other object besides those, the response is yes, in the sense that one can speak of the various components of the basis of designation or of the designating mind. However, to think that out there in objective reality there is any object that exists in and of itself is entirely wrong.

In Buddhist terminology the term "object" (Tib. *yul*) and the term "phenomenon" (Tib. *chos*) are mutually inclusive: anything that is an object is necessarily a phenomenon, and anything that is a phenomenon is necessarily an object. However, if two phenomena are of the same nature, this does not mean that they are necessarily mutually inclusive. Mutual inclusivity of A and B means that if something is the A, it must be B, and if something is the B, it must be A. For example, we can say that a basis of designation is of the same nature as an object, for there is no basis of designation that is not an object. However, if something is an object, it is not necessarily a basis of designation. Those two are not mutually inclusive. There are many objects that are not bases of designation. For instance, Buddhism is an object but, taken by itself, it is not a basis of designation.

The entire universe and everything in it is conceptually designated. The *sūtras* state that all these phenomena are designated by thoughts. They do not say they are designated by awareness. This does not imply that it is possible for there to be thoughts in the absence of awareness. Consider the significance of the statement in the *sūtras* that all phenomena are designated by thought, but not that they are designated by awareness. Why do you think that is said? The *sūtras* say that a *buddha* perceives all phenomena as clearly as an ordinary person sees something in the palm of his hand, and that a *buddha* perceives all phenomena as being of "one taste."

Consider the question of whether it is possible to perceive phenomena prior to conceptual designation. There is no limit to conceptual designation. One could almost say that the *buddhas* and conceptualization come into existence simultaneously. To posit the existence of phenomena that exist independently of conceptual designation, we would need some compelling evidence for their existence. We say that phenomena are established by the power of conceptual designation.

If there were some entity that existed independently of the power of conceptual designation, then that entity would be truly existent. Needless to say, if that were the case, the whole theory of emptiness would be in deep trouble.

Personal and Phenomenal Identitylessness

Concerning the two types of identitylessness, namely personal identitylessness (Tib. *gang zag gi bdag med*) and phenomenal identitylessness (Tib. *chos kyi bdag med*), there is no difference in the nature of the object to be refuted. The distinction between these two types of emptiness is only in terms of the bases of emptiness. In what sense does one speak of the bases of emptiness? It is upon such a basis that there is an object of refutation. One establishes personal identitylessness by establishing emptiness upon the basis of a person. On the other hand, one establishes phenomenal identitylessness by establishing emptiness upon the basis of some phenomenon other than a person. Thus, the absence of true existence of a person is called personal identitylessness, while the absence of true existence of any other phenomenon is called phenomenal identitylessness.

Emptiness with reference to the aggregates is an instance of phenomenal identitylessness, whereas the absence of true existence of a person—such as a human or an animal—is an instance of personal identitylessness. Similarly one can even speak of the lack of true existence of a *buddha*; this too is an instance of personal identitylessness. But the emptiness realized on the basis of anything other than persons or sentient beings is phenomenal identitylessness.

CHICAGO STATE ST - 312-279-2133
1 S STATE ST
CHICAGO, IL 60603
01/28/2019 06:43 PM EXPIRES 04/28/19

GROCERY
212060006   MP OLIVES   FB $1.49
   MP OLIVES   OLIVE STFD PIM 5.75OZ

                          SUBTOTAL $1.49
B = IL TAX 2.2500% on $1.49 $0.03

                            TOTAL $1.52
  *6087 DEBIT TOTAL PAYMENT $1.52
              AID: A0000000980840
              US DEBIT

REC#2-9028-2799-0169-1125-4 VCD#752-285-752

Chapter Five

The Prāsaṅgika View
of How Phenomena Exist

The reasoning discussed in the previous chapter leads to the conclusion that the self does not exist inherently. So how does the self exist? The answer to this is that the self exists by the power of convention. Since phenomena do not exist inherently, they must exist conventionally. And since phenomena are established by the power of convention, they exist in a dependent fashion. Phenomena are dependent upon something else; in particular, they are dependent upon conceptual designation.

There are a number of Buddhist scriptures that make this point. For example, there are *sūtras* that say phenomena are established by conception. Also, Nāgārjuna's writings say that phenomena are established by thought, and Āryadeva makes the same point. All these Buddhist writings say that phenomena are established by convention, and what they mean here is that they are conceptually designated.

This is an assertion unique to the Prāsaṅgika Madhyamaka view. All four Buddhist philosophical systems affirm that phenomena are dependent upon the collection of their preceding causes and conditions. But apart from the Prāsaṅgika system, the other Buddhist philosophical systems do not assert that phenomena are established by conception. Advocates of those other systems are not able to comprehend this point.

Everything that exists appears to the mind as if it were inherently existent. These other systems assume that if something does not inherently exist, it must be utterly nonexistent. One can ask whether true existence is something that is established by thought. Is a blue mountain something established by thought? Similarly, are people and sentient beings alike in the sense of being established by thought? The answer to that question is that they are all alike in that they are all conceptually designated.

THREE CRITERIA FOR DESIGNATING
THE EXISTENCE OF PHENOMENA

Now we can ask a further question: if something is conceptually designated, is it therefore existent, or may it be nonexistent? It is said that a blue mountain does not exist. Given that all entities are conceptually designated, what is the criterion for determining what does and does not exist? We say that a blue mountain is conceptually designated, but it does not exist. What do we mean by that? It means that a deluded person affirms its existence. And we say that a mountain is conceptually designated and that moreover it exists by being established by conceptual designation. The distinction here comes from the fact that three qualities all need to come together for something to exist by way of being conceptually designated.

The first criterion is that the phenomenon has to be commonly accepted with respect to ordinary cognition (Tib. *tha mal pa'i shes pa la grags pa*). True existence is something that is consensually accepted by people's ordinary cognitions, and other nonexistent things are as well. This word "consensual" simply means "accepted by ordinary awareness."

The second criterion is that the phenomenon must not be repudiated by conventional cognition (Tib. *tha snyad pa'i shes pas mi gnod pa*). For example, the awareness that cognizes a blue mountain is undermined by the awareness that cognizes a white mountain, which invalidates the awareness of the blue snow mountain. On the contrary, while the white snow mountain is also something that is conceptually designated, the awareness of the white snow mountain is not invalidated by any other awareness. Since it is not undermined by any conventional awareness, we can therefore say that it exists.

The third criterion is that the phenomenon is also not repudiated by reasoning that investigates ultimate reality (Tib. *de kho nyid kyi rigs pas kyang mi gnod pa*). This means that the phenomenon in question is not invalidated by an awareness that investigates emptiness. True existence is something that cannot be repudiated by conventional awareness. Conventional awareness is an awareness that has as its object a conventional reality. However, true existence is something that is repudiated by an awareness that realizes emptiness. When we say that ignorance apprehends true existence, what it is apprehending is inherent existence. If phenomena were truly, or inherently, existent, then that would be their ultimate mode of existence. The awareness that realizes the ultimate mode of being of phenomena is the awareness that realizes emptiness. But this awareness, rather than realizing true existence, realizes the very absence of true existence.

Let's take a specific example. The flower I'm holding in my hand is something that is accepted by the ordinary mind. And why is that? Because we agree that it is a flower. Moreover, there is no conventional awareness that sees this as not a flower. The fact that this is a flower is not repudiated by any conventional awareness. If this flower were truly existent, then it would have to be observed by the mind that realizes emptiness. However, when we seek out the true existence of the flower, such true existence is not to be found. So it does exist, but its existence is necessarily conventional.

Conventional existence is not repudiated by the awareness that investigates ultimate reality. The wisdom that investigates ultimate reality repudiates true existence but not conventional existence. Therefore, according to the Prāsaṅgika system, the

above three criteria must be satisfied in order to establish that
something is existent. Meanwhile, assertions such as those
made by the Svātantrika Madhyamaka system, the Cittamātra
system, and the Sautrāntika and Vaibhāṣika systems are repudiated by the wisdom that investigates ultimate reality. The
Svātantrika Madhyamaka view maintains that something exists by its own characteristics; the Cittamātra view asserts the
true existence of a total-ground consciousness (Tib. *kun gzhi'i
rnam par shes pa*); and both the Sautrāntika and Vaibhāṣika
systems assert that impermanent phenomena truly exist. All
such assertions, according to the Prāsaṅgika view, are repudiated by the wisdom that investigates ultimate reality. All
those other Buddhist philosophical systems affirm that phenomena exist by their own characteristics, and they all find it
impossible to establish the existence of a phenomenon unless
it exists by its own characteristics. So the Prāsaṅgika view that
phenomena are simply conceptually designated—that they
do not exist from their own side—repudiates this view held
by all the other Buddhist philosophical systems.

Tsongkhapa comments that a pot is conceptually designated in the same way that a snake is conceptually designated
on the basis of a mottled rope. That is, the process of conceptual designation in these two cases is just the same. But, he
continues, there is a distinction. In terms of the conventional
existence of the snake versus the pot, there is a difference in
terms of whether the snake and the pot are able to perform
the functions of those designated entities. The snake that is
designated upon the mottled rope is not able to perform the
functions of a snake; it is not able to act like a snake. The pot,
on the other hand, is able to perform the functions of a pot.
Moreover, the mode of ascertaining the snake designated upon
the mottled rope and the mode of ascertaining the pot are
also very different. Moreover, the ascertainment of the snake
designated upon the mottled rope and the ascertainment of the
pot are also completely different with respect to their vulner-
ability to being repudiated. Since these are the three criteria

that must be satisfied in order to establish something as being conventionally existent, the pot is conventionally existent but the snake is not.

Moreover, there is a statement in *A Guide to the Bodhisattva Way of Life* (IX: 25) to the effect that the objects of sensory perceptions are not refuted or negated by an understanding of emptiness. This same statement is also implied by the aforementioned three criteria for establishing conventional existence. For example, the statement that a snow mountain is something conceptually designated does not repudiate the assertion that the snow mountain seen by the eye is in fact a snow mountain. So what is repudiated by the wisdom that realizes emptiness? Such wisdom realizes that the basis, namely the mountain, has no true existence. It repudiates the notion of that basis as truly existent. Still, the wisdom that realizes emptiness does not repudiate the existence of phenomena that are accepted by ordinary awareness. Those various sensory objects are not repudiated by ordinary awareness, nor by reasoning that investigates conventional reality, nor by reasoning that investigates ultimate reality. So in this way the statement from *A Guide to the Bodhisattva Way of Life* and the three criteria for the conventional existence are in complete agreement.

There are some Gelugpa scholars who add a fourth criterion for establishing conventional existence, namely that the phenomenon must have a valid basis of designation (Tib. *gdags gzhi tshad ma*). This fourth criterion of a valid basis of designation is not stated by Tsongkhapa. Nowhere in any of the writings of Tsongkhapa does one find any reference to a so-called valid basis of designation. The assertion of this fourth criterion implies that its advocates are still grasping onto phenomena existing by their own characteristics. They are not satisfied that there isn't some qualifier from the object's side, from the side of the basis of designation. So they add this qualifier that there must be a *valid* basis of designation. Before a designation is made, any kind of basis of designation will do.

There can be no distinction between a valid and an invalid basis of designation. We can make any designation we like. There is nothing that can repudiate the designation we make. As I mentioned earlier, there is a designation by thought, but once that designation is made, we simply need to learn what that designation is.

If the aforementioned three criteria for conventional existence are satisfied, then we say that something exists, whereas if these criteria are not met, then we cannot establish that something as existing. Therefore, the conventional agreement of conceptual designation and the question of whether or not they are subject to repudiation have to be determined with respect to individual communities. Each instance must be judged on the basis of conventional usage in each community or each society. The individual conventional agreements within each society determine whether or not something can be repudiated by conventional awareness. The power really lies in the conventional agreement of a society.

When the Chinese first came to Tibet, there was in Tibet itself no custom whatsoever for clapping one's hands in applause. Traditionally, the only time when Tibetans clap their hands is when they find something absolutely amazing, although clapping does have one other symbolic significance: it symbolizes the complete annihilation of something. When the Chinese gave lectures to the Tibetans, they told the Tibetans to applaud by clapping their hands. When the Chinese gave the people political propaganda, the Tibetans very gladly complied with much laughter. The Tibetans were delighted to clap their hands, and the Chinese too enjoyed this response.

Another example is that in traditional Tibetan culture, when you put your thumb up in the air, this shows that you are asking for a favor. Another symbolic significance of raising the thumb is to show that something is really first rate. However, if you make the same gesture of sticking up your thumb to the Bhutanese, or to Asian Indians, then they interpret this to mean that you should eat excrement. Clearly there are different kinds of conventional agreements from one society to another. Another example is that in Tibet, if a person is given a paper hat to wear, this shows that this person is to be banished from a given region. Meanwhile, in the United States, children are given paper hats to wear at birthday parties. Wearing a paper hat means two very different things in these two contexts. Yet another example comes from one of my first experiences in the United States. The day after I arrived in the United States, I was taken out to a picnic, and during this picnic a number of children came up to me and said "Hi!" Now in Tibet, if you say "Hi" to someone, it is rather insulting. I then asked Alan what is meant by this word "Hi," and he responded that it is a friendly way of greeting someone. It is important not to mix up the conventions of one society with those of another, otherwise you find that the conventions of one society will impinge upon the conventions of the other. In these cases of inter-societal exchanges, the fact that these are purely conceptual designations becomes extremely clear. There is nothing good or bad objectively in these gestures and phrases. Their goodness or badness comes purely out of social, or consensual, agreement.

This becomes very evident, for example, when one sees in theaters, in music, or in dance, the types of ornaments and clothing that are worn from one society to another. On the one hand one sees great differences, yet in each society the modes of dancing, singing, acting, and so forth are all regarded as very attractive. All this comes by the power of familiarization: we become accustomed to a particular fashion, but this all comes about by conceptual designation. Nothing is either good or bad objectively about any of these fashions. When Tibetan refugees first came down to India and heard the Indians singing, the Tibetans thought that the Indians were crying. And similarly the Indians thought the Tibetans were wailing when they heard them singing. But each society finds its own way of singing very melodious. What we find attractive or unattractive, good or bad, as exemplified by these instances, stems purely from what we are accustomed to. If we examine the differences in cultural norms from one society to another, then the fact that they are all conceptually designated becomes very evident.

HOW ALL PHENOMENA APPEAR LIKE ILLUSIONS

I would now like to discuss how a person has an illusion-like existence. In order for something to appear like an illusion, two cognitions are needed. One is the awareness of the *appearance* of the phenomenon, and the other is an awareness that despite appearances, the phenomenon does not truly exist. In other words, the phenomenon does not exist in the manner in which it appears. With those two types of cognition, one realizes that the appearance is misleading.

For example, in the case of a magical apparition of horses and elephants, there may be an awareness that recognizes that these are purely illusions. In addition, there may be a recognition that in fact there are no horses and elephants there. With these two types of awareness, one determines that the appearance of horses and elephants is illusory. Whatever phenomena we observe, they all appear as if they were truly existent. This applies to all animate and inanimate phenomena. The only mode of appearance that we experience is the mode of appearance of phenomena as truly existent.

For all sentient beings—except those who are fully enlightened and who directly, nonconceptually realize emptiness— all conventional reality appears as if phenomena were truly existent. It is crucial to understand what we mean when we say there is an appearance of true existence. If the phenomenon appears as if it were truly existent, it appears as if it existed independently of any kind of labeling, as if it existed independently of the basis of its characteristics, and as if it existed independently of its characteristics. When the "I" appears to the mind as being truly existent, it appears to exist in and of itself. That is the appearance of true existence.

It is very important for us to recognize the manner in which phenomena appear as truly existent. But now we need to ask whether phenomena actually exist in this fashion. In terms of the mode of being of phenomena, they exist in dependence upon the assembly of many factors, but they appear as if they exist independently of those other factors.

At first there is the awareness of the appearance of phenomena as if they did not depend upon any components. But at second glance, the awareness that realizes identitylessness may arise, which recognizes that phenomena do not truly exist in the manner in which they appear. In dependence upon these two types of cognition, one realizes the lack of true existence and the deceptive, illusory-like nature of phenomena. Returning to the analogy of the magician who conjures up horses and elephants, there is first the awareness of an appearance of horses and elephants, and then there is the awareness that the appearance of horses and elephants is deceptive. These two types of cognition are indispensable. If one has only an awareness of true existence, then that awareness would not be sufficient for realizing that these appearances are false, or deceptive. For the mind that has sought the truly existent self within the basis of designation and not found it, there is no appearance of a truly existent self.

THE DEPENDENCE OF PHENOMENA

The self depends for its existence upon conceptual designation, but what else does the "I" depend upon? To give an analogy, we can point to offering bowls resting on an altar. Those offering bowls on the altar depend on the altar. What is meant by saying that these bowls on the altar depend on the altar? What is meant by this word "depend"? Were that altar not there, there could be no bowls resting on it. When we speak of A depending on B, this means that the presence or absence of A depends upon the presence or absence of B. Were B not there, then A could not be there. The bowls on the altar are not something independent, or self-sufficient. Whenever you hear this word "dependent" in a Buddhist context, this is how you should understand it.

There are two types of dependence. One is a temporary dependence, while the other is an invariable dependence. An example of an invariable dependence occurs in the case of a sprout, since a sprout is always dependent for its production upon a seed. The dependence of these bowls on the altar is something temporary. For those bowls to be on the altar, of course, there must be an altar, but this is a temporary dependence. Clearly there does not need to be an altar for there to be bowls.

Similarly, my presence right now in this house depends on this house. Were this house not here, then I could not be here. But generally my existence does not depend on this room. Rather, my existence depends upon conceptualization. If there were no conceptualization, I would not exist. Therefore, when we say something is dependent, it means it is fabricated. It is dependent for its very existence upon something else. As soon as we assert that something is dependent upon other things, this immediately implies that it does not inherently exist.

Let's take human beings as an example. It seems almost as if the world in which we dwell is dependent for its existence upon our existence. For example, if we had no eyes, if we had no visual perception, then it would be just about impossible to establish the existence of our known world: all visual forms, shapes, and colors would vanish. If we were to lack tactile sensations, or the feeling of touch, then it would be impossible for us to establish the existence of tangible objects: there would be no solidity, heat, cold, and so forth. If we had no auditory perception, it would be impossible for us to establish the presence of sound. Were we to have no gustatory awareness, there would be no tastes. And with no olfactory awareness, there would be no smells. And were we to have no visual awareness, then the intervening space between ourselves and other things could not be established as existent.

In Buddhism we speak of intervening space, which is something seen by the visual awareness. But we also speak of noncomposite space, which is not visually seen, but is described as the sheer absence of tangible obstruction. Were we to have no tactile awareness, then it would be impossible for us to establish the presence or absence of a tangible obstruction, in which case it also would be impossible to establish the presence of noncomposite space. Therefore, it seems that our five types of sensory awareness in fact fabricate the world of animate and inanimate objects. Hence, the world that we experience depends for its existence upon our five types of sensory awareness. This is why we can conclude that there are no independent, objective phenomena.

Now, we experience a variety of sensory appearances, and in accordance with individual societies—that is, the customs and conventional agreements of specific societies—these various appearances are labeled in diverse ways. They are conceptually designated in various ways, and then the objects that are so designated perform the functions for which they were designated. Likewise, external phenomena, phenomena out in the world, are dependently existent. For example, we have such pairs as high and low. It is impossible to establish one without the other. The same holds true for good and bad, short and long, darkness and light, outside and inside, and so forth: all such objects designated in any of these ways are clearly dependent upon their opposites. We cannot establish light without dark. These are just a few examples, but this principle holds for all phenomena without exception. With the arising of manifold appearances, we conceptually designate these appearances in manifold ways, so we can conclude that phenomena are created by conceptual designation.

To counter the objection that even if we were blind, forms would still exist, we need to understand that a blind person wouldn't be able to establish the color of a flower. Moreover, if this blind person were to have no tactile awareness, it would be impossible for this person to establish any kind of shape of the flower either. If the person had no tactile awareness, it would be impossible for the person to observe the flower. Of course, someone else could describe the flower to the blind person, but in order to understand the explanation, the person would have to have auditory awareness. Moreover, if this person were born blind, how could someone else explain to that person that the flower is red and not black? If the person had no tactile awareness, how could anyone describe its shape to that person? It could be described as round, but what is round? Something that is not square? If it is white, does it help to say that it is not green? And even the presence of this explainer, this companion to the blind person, can only be established if the blind person has some sensory awareness. For example, the shape and the color of the explainer's body are fabricated by visual awareness. The sound of the explainer's voice is created by auditory awareness. And the tactile qualities of the explainer's body are created by tactile awareness. The lack of sensory faculties really leaves people on their own. What is left in the absence of sensory awareness? There one is, simply by oneself. The individual, the person, is the creator of the world. In fact, the very notion of a divine Creator is also something of our own creation.

The presence of a flower can be established only in dependence upon visual awareness, and likewise the shape and color of a flower can be established only in dependence upon the visual awareness. So we say that it is fabricated by visual awareness. That is what we mean by fabricated, or created. The products created by a carpenter are created in dependence upon a carpenter and the carpenter's usage of certain tools, so we say that the carpenter creates his products. Similarly, the shape and the color of a flower, for example, are created by visual awareness.

While it is said that all phenomena exist in dependence upon conceptual designation, one may wonder, "Isn't it possible that there are some appearances that exist without conceptual designation?" Don't certain appearances arise whether or not there is any conceptual designation? Actually, the very arising of appearances themselves depends on other things. The very fact of appearance is dependent upon the fact of nonappearance. Were there no such concept as nonappearance, it would be impossible to establish an appearance. For even if we have the sense that something appears prior to conceptual designation, the sheer fact that it appears to consciousness already implies that conceptual designation has taken place. Investigate this nature of dependence, the manner in which thought designates phenomena, and the manner in which phenomena do not exist inherently, and train in this way.

THE CRITERIA FOR REALIZING EMPTINESS

What is the criterion by which one judges whether or not emptiness is realized? Having sought out the designated object, one does not find it. At first one is not satisfied with the idea that a phenomenon is simply conceptually designated, so one analytically seeks out the designated object, but then recognizes that the designated object is not findable under analysis. And the very recognition of the absence of such a designated object constitutes the realization of emptiness. So it is fairly easy to get that type of certainty. For example, if you tell me, "You are a terrible person," then the sense of "I" arises very tangibly. Then I can examine within my body, within the five appendages of my body, and within the mind to see if there is anything corresponding to that sense of a tangible, truly existent self. Through this process I will recognize that there is no self of that sort. It is relatively easy. By realizing this, I can understand that it is purely by means of conventional agreement that I can establish my own existence, that I can still engage in action, and that I can experience the results of my actions. If in this life I engage in virtuous actions, in the future I will take a fortunate rebirth, but if I engage in nonvirtuous actions, then in the future I will gain an miserable rebirth. By realizing the conventional nature of my existence, I can realize that phrases such as "I am doing this," "I am going here," "I experience this," and "I want this," can all be established very comfortably, purely as conceptual designations. If one fathoms this, one realizes emptiness.

However, if you cannot integrate both aspects—the assertion that there is no truly existent self, but that it is perfectly valid to say "I am doing this," "I am going there," "I want that," and so forth on a purely conventional basis—if you have not established those two, then you have not realized emptiness. Through the first assertion, one avoids the extreme of substantialism, and through the second assertion one avoids the extreme of nihilism.

On the one hand, you may engage in an analysis that should lead you to refute inherent existence, but you may still feel that there must be something there from the side of the basis of designation or the object, and you may not be able to let go of this. If this happens, it means that you have not been able to fully counteract the mode of apprehension of ignorance, so you fall into the extreme of substantialism, which is counteracted by the recognition that there is no truly existent self.

On the other hand, the second assertion of the validity of statements such as "I am speaking" suggests that a purely conventionally established self can perform all the functions of a person. But you may be unable to establish the conventional existence of phenomena, due to realizing the absence, or unfindability, of the designated objects; that may lead you to conclude that they are nonexistent. If this happens, then you are not able to establish the fact that a conventionally existent "I" is able to perform all the functions of the self, and you fall into the extreme of nihilism. The assertion that such statements concerning a conventional "I" are valid statements counteracts the extreme of nihilism. It is said that in order to realize emptiness, one must be free of these two extremes.

Counter-intuitive as it may seem, it is also said that when one understands emptiness, one's awareness of appearances should dispel the reified extreme of existence and one's awareness of emptiness should dispel the reified extreme of nonexistence. If one examines the mode of appearance of something like a flower, that very examination frees one from the extreme of existence, which is identical to the extreme of substantialism. How is this so? As one examines the appearance of something like the flower, one sees that there are three factors involved. There is the appearance of the flower, there is its mode of appearance, and there is that to which it appears, such as the visual awareness. Seeing the interdependence of these three leads to the certainty that the appearing object is not intrinsically, or inherently, existent.

When we say that emptiness dispels the nihilistic extreme, we mean that the very fact that phenomena do not inherently exist frees us from that extreme. If the flower, for instance, is empty of inherent existence, this already implies that it is dependent upon something else. Although it is not inherently existent, it exists in a dependent fashion.

Here is another point to consider: Emptiness appears as a dependently related event, and dependently related events appear as emptiness. This means that dependent origination appears as the meaning of emptiness. Thus, the ascertainment that phenomena exist in a dependent fashion is complementary to the ascertainment that phenomena do not inherently exist. Not only does the former not repudiate the latter, but rather, it complements it. Similarly, the ascertainment that phenomena do not inherently exist complements the ascertainment that phenomena exist in a dependent fashion. One does not repudiate the other; rather, they complement one another.

The mind that ascertains the nonexistence of a blue snow mountain repudiates the awareness that affirms the existence of a blue snow mountain. These two do not complement each other; they repudiate each other. In contrast, the mind that ascertains the lack of inherent existence of phenomena does not repudiate the ascertainment that phenomena exist in a dependent fashion, but complements it. In fact, Nāgārjuna states that to the person for whom emptiness is possible, all phenomena are possible. To the person for whom emptiness is impossible all phenomena are impossible. This statement establishes the complementary nature of these two realizations: the realization of the dependent nature of phenomena and the realization of their lack of true existence.

You may ask, "If I were to inherently existent, would it be possible for me to engage in action?" The answer is no, for you would be immutable. Only if I am not inherently existent am I able to engage in actions. If something exists in a dependent fashion, conventionally, and one realizes this, then it is easy to realize that the phenomenon does not inherently exist. Moreover, if something existed that did not depend upon anything else, then one would not be able to establish its lack of inherent existence. So for the very reason that phenomena are not inherently existent, it follows that they exist in a dependent fashion. And by existing conventionally, but not inherently, one can engage in action.

This is about all I wish to say about realizing emptiness. I could go on to explain the refutation of phenomena arising following any one of the four extremes, namely, "Not from self, not from other, not from both, not without cause, whatever phenomena arise never has birth been of those four" (Tib. *bdag las ma yin/ gzhan las min/ gnyis las ma yin/ rgyu med min/ dngos po gang dang gang na yang/ skye ba nam yang yod ma yin*). But this is not so important, and we have implicitly covered it already. The gist of that analysis is that in any of those cases, by seeking the designated object, true existence is repudiated.

To make one final comment, when I speak of the dependence of physical objects upon sensory awareness, I am not suggesting that a flower is dependent upon any particular individual's awareness. It is dependent upon sensory awareness in general. But it can still be said that the flower that appears to your awareness is dependent on your awareness.

If you examine this issue very closely, you are led to the conclusion that the world that appears to you actually does not appear to anyone else. This implies that the world that each of us lives in is in fact produced by our own sensory awareness. This has a direct bearing on the issue of pure vision (Tib. *dag snang*) in Buddhism. By the very process of purifying one's own mind, the appearance of the world is also purified. And as you experience a pure vision of the world, the whole world in which you dwell becomes transformed. In this regard we say that the whole world arises as the result of maturation of the habitual propensities. In this way the world is like a dream.

Let us dedicate the merit of this teaching so that all sentient beings may realize emptiness and attain perfect spiritual awakening. May the teachings of the Buddha flourish, may our spiritual teachers live long, and may all sentient beings experience both temporal as well as ultimate happiness.

Appendix I
Dzogchen

A *sūtra* states that all phenomena arise from conditions. One can interpret this to mean that all phenomena of joy and of sorrow arise in dependence upon conditions. Or in the term "all phenomena" one can include all factors that lead to the attainment of full awakening, as well as all other phenomena within the cycle of existence. All the phenomena leading to awakening depend upon yearning, faith, and confidence. This implies that the question of whether an action is virtuous or nonvirtuous is determined by the motivation that impels it. If the motivation is wholesome, then the ensuing verbal or physical actions are bound to be wholesome, and if the motivation is unwholesome, then the verbal and physical action will also be unwholesome.

Whether or not one's practice is indeed a Mahāyāna practice depends upon one's motivation, specifically upon whether or not the motivation is a spirit of awakening, moved by compassion and altruism. Likewise, whether or not one's actions actually do lead to liberation depends upon whether or not they are motivated by a spirit of emergence. Furthermore, if one's practice is to be regarded as that of a person of small capacity, one's motivation must be concerned with one's own well-being beyond this lifetime alone. If one's motivation for practice is concerned exclusively with trying to find some happiness and alleviate one's suffering in this lifetime, then such practice is not even that of a person of small capacity. Thus, one's motivation is very, very important.

One's intention is instrumental in determining whether any type of action is accomplished and how it is accomplished. In order to establish one's well-being in future lives, one's motivation must be wholesome, even though this is not always the case for purely mundane activities concerned with this life alone. Thus, please cultivate the most wholesome motivation you can as you engage with the following material.

All Buddhist Dharma—including that written in Buddhist scriptures as well as the Dharma of realization—have compassion as their root. Thus, there is a strong emphasis in Buddhism on the need to relieve and protect others from suffering. Buddhist Dharma includes Hīnayāna teachings, which pertain to the practices of persons of small and medium capacities, and Buddhist Dharma includes Mahāyāna teachings. In both of these contexts there is a very strong emphasis on not inflicting harm upon others. As the motivation to avoid harming others arises, that leads to compassion, too.

The cultivation of compassion is really a priceless means for bringing about genuine happiness. In the absence of compassion, even if actions have the appearance of compassion, whatever one does is bound to bring trouble to oneself and others. So, doesn't compassion seem to be a great source of refuge for all sentient beings? If we show compassion toward others, what is the result of that? It brings others happiness and protects them from suffering. Likewise, if others show compassion toward us, what is the result? We too are given happiness and our suffering is alleviated.

In this life we have obtained a human life and have had the opportunity to encounter the Dharma, so we have attained what is called a fully endowed human life. How can we take the essence of this opportunity? How can we make this precious human life most meaningful? The most essential point is cultivating compassion. If we fail to cultivate compassion, it is very difficult to bring any benefit or be of true service to other sentient beings. In short, compassion is extremely important for all of humanity. In this world of strife the only key is compassion. If there is no compassion, there is simply no way that these problems can be alleviated.

I would now like to address the practice of meditative quiescence (Tib. *zhi gnas*) focused upon the mind itself, and to explain the method of practice called Dzogchen, or the Great Perfection.

In his text *An Ornament for the Sūtras (Sūtrālaṃkāra)* Maitreya comments that one should recognize one's affliction. This is a metaphor of the patient, the doctor and the medicine, and the joy of being healed; it implies that one should not simply tolerate one's ailments. This can be related to the Four Noble Truths and to the process of revolving in the cycle of existence. The essence of this whole process is the truths of suffering and the source of suffering. When Maitreya speaks of not tolerating one's ailment, that means recognizing the source of one's suffering and not putting up with it. As long as our minds are dominated by mental afflictions, there is really no opportunity for a lasting state of well-being. This needs to be recognized. As long as we do not become disillusioned with this state of affairs, the desire to find relief and to eliminate the sources of suffering will not arise.

In order to be freed from illness, one needs to eliminate the cause of the illness. This is analogous to the first two of the Four Noble Truths. If one is unhappy about the reality of suffering, one needs to abandon the source of suffering, which is the Second Noble Truth. There are two aspects to the source of suffering: mental afflictions and the actions, known as *karma*, that are incited by mental afflictions. What we seek is the genuine happiness of being free from those afflictions.

The goals of the practice are to be freed from the reality of suffering and the afflictive obscurations that lie at its source—in other words to attain *nirvāṇa*—and to be freed from the most subtle cognitive obscurations, thereby attaining perfect spiritual awakening. One should practice meditation as an antidote to those obscurations. Just as it is impossible to be healed from a serious illness without taking medication, so it is not possible to gain release from the source of suffering without applying oneself to practices that counteract the source of suffering. Whether one is following practices taught in the *sūtras* or the *tantras*, in the context of Buddhism the essential structure of practice boils down to the Four Noble Truths.

Among the two aspects of the source of suffering—mental afflictions and the actions that are incited by those afflictions—mental afflictions are primary, for in their absence, *karma* does not ensue. There are a variety of mental afflictions—including pride, attachment, anger, competitiveness, and jealousy—but the one root for all of them is ignorance. If we can eliminate this ignorance, the other mental afflictions will vanish.

In order to cut ignorance, or "non-awareness," at its very root, the Three Higher Trainings are taught, namely, ethical discipline, meditative concentration, and wisdom. These are included in the Truth of the Path, the Fourth Noble Truth. In the context of the Dzogchen tradition, what is the method for cutting away the root of ignorance? It is called awareness. According the *sūtra* teachings within Buddhism, it is the wisdom that realizes emptiness that cuts the root of ignorance. How do these two statements relate to the Three Higher Trainings? They both pertain to the training in wisdom, which needs to be supported by meditative concentration.

In the teachings on the actual practice of Dzogchen, there is no explicit reference to the cultivation of meditative quiescence, or concentration, as a separate discipline, though it is said that one needs to attend continually to the nature of one's own awareness. It is impossible to do that unless one has achieved some degree of attentional stability. The *sūtras* explicitly discuss the cultivation of meditative concentration, which is often referred to as quiescence. In order to cultivate quiescence, one must begin by cultivating ethical discipline; otherwise, the training in meditative concentration will not succeed. So ethical discipline is the foundation on which one then cultivates quiescence.

Within the actual practice of quiescence, one may focus on any of a wide variety of meditative objects. The method that I would like to discuss now entails focusing the attention upon the mind itself. The methods taught in Dzogchen teachings have a great deal in common with the quiescence practice of attending to the mind itself. The *sūtras* state that in order to stabilize the mind by directing the attention to the mind itself, six prerequisites must be satisfied. If one wholeheartedly wishes to apply oneself to the attainment of authentic quiescence, then it is imperative to satisfy these six preliminary conditions. I have discussed these six in my earlier book *Calming the Mind* (Ithaca: Snow Lion Publications, 1995).

In this regard, it is imperative to know how mental afflictions arise and how to counter them. In this practice one must ascertain the essential characteristics of the mind and then focus one's attention upon the mind. However, at the beginning it is quite difficult to correctly recognize the essential characteristics of the mind. Success generally comes about only by familiarizing oneself with the practice, and by gaining experience in it.

To understand what is meant by the terms "mind," "cognition," and "awareness," one must first comprehend that we as human beings have what are called the five aggregates. Among those aggregates there is the capacity for the arising of appearances and the capacity for the apprehension of appearances. In the *sūtras*, that capacity, both for the arising of appearances and the apprehension of appearances, is given the name "awareness."

What is the actual nature of this awareness? It is luminosity and cognition. Let's look first of all at this quality of luminosity.

There are two types of luminosity. There is the other-directed luminosity and there is the self-directed, or internal, luminosity. An outer phenomenon, such as a lamp, has the capacity of other-directed luminosity but not self-directed luminosity. An external example of something that has internal luminosity is a mirror, which has a limpid quality, that allows for the appearance of reflections or images. Now look to your own experience, as various images or appearances come to the mind. There has to be some basis for these appearances. Likewise, there has to be some basis for the images that appear in the mirror.

After focusing in meditation on the limpid, luminous quality of the mind, when one concludes the session, one should direct the attention back to one's previous meditative state, which may enable one to sustain that awareness of the limpid, luminous quality of awareness. By cultivating quiescence by focusing upon the mind, after awhile one is able to ascertain the primary qualities of awareness of the mind itself, namely luminosity and cognition, which yields insight into the conventional nature of the mind. In contrast, in the genuine practice of Dzogchen, one experiences the ultimate nature of the mind. Dodrubchen, a great nineteenth-century Dzogchen master, states that the primordial clear light that is realized in tantric systems such as Cakrasaṃvara and Guhyasamāja is identical with the awareness that is realized in the practice of Dzogchen. The actual methods of practice are different, but they lead to the same result.

Modern scientists say that mindfulness of appearances arises in dependence upon the brain, but it is difficult for them to say exactly what the mind and awareness are. For example, if we recall a person whom we have encountered sometime in the past, and some image of that person appears to our mind's eye, there has to be a basis for that image to arise, and that basis is called awareness. In terms of the external example of a mirror, it provides a basis for those images to appear, but what is absent in the mirror is cognition. Thus, a mirror has a luminous quality, but, unlike the mind, it lacks cognition. The mind is endowed with luminosity and cognition. In practice you should experientially ascertain these essential qualities of the mind—clarity and cognition—and place your attention on those very features.

Because the mind is not a physical phenomenon, it seems to have no borders. For example, although I am now sitting in a rather small room, I can direct my awareness to our galaxy, and some type of generic idea of the galaxy does appear, even though I am sitting in this room. When I simply sit here and mentally direct my attention to all the cardinal directions, up and down, and mentally expand my awareness out to any limit of space, it really seems that awareness itself is co-existent with space. And it is said that this is actually true in reality.

It takes some understanding to distinguish between awareness and conceptualization. It is said that the scope of conceptualization is very limited, whereas awareness pervades all that exists. This is true of the awareness of each sentient being; each one pervades all that exists. The point of this meditation practice is to ascertain the nature of the mind and then simply sustain one's attention in that realization. But it is difficult to actually realize the nature of the mind in practice.

In many Buddhist treatises it is said that awareness dwells within one's body, so how does this relate to the above assertion that awareness pervades all that exists? Dodrubchen draws a distinction between the location of awareness and its manifestation. There is also a distinction between the pervasiveness of awareness throughout all of existence and its manifestation. In the culmination of Dzogchen practice, when awareness manifests, all phenomena are exhausted and the mind (Tib. *sems*) also vanishes. When awareness manifests, there is nothing to adopt and nothing to abandon. However, before awareness manifests, that is, while conceptualization still exists, if one does not follow the law of *karma*, abandoning the unwholesome and adopting the wholesome, one will never realize the essential nature of awareness and experience its manifestation.

On a very practical level, the meditation can begin with a simple awareness of the breath. This is especially beneficial if the conceptual mind is very turbulent, which makes it difficult to observe the mind itself. In order to subdue the conceptual turbulence, breath awareness is recommended. Now it is very important to develop a resolve during this meditation period to maintain that presence of awareness, and not let the mind become distracted. During the meditation session, as various thoughts and appearances arise, it is very important not to identify with them and follow after them. Rather, one should release them and then rest in that state. According to the *sūtras*, this practice is called the cultivation of quiescence focused upon the mind.

Dzogchen practice can be regarded as part of tantric practice, which of course is to be taught only to those who are qualified. However, I feel that nothing I discuss here needs to be held secret or should not be explained to a general audience. According to the Dzogchen teachings, the nature of the awareness completely saturates all conceptualization and all objects of conceptualization. According to some lineages of the Dzogchen teachings, it is said that between one thought and the next, awareness manifests. I have already discussed the nature of awareness according to the *sūtras*, and apart from the subtlety of awareness discussed in the Dzogchen tradition, the nature of awareness is as I described it earlier.

Nāgārjuna comments that total emptiness, or universal emptiness, remains upon the complete cessation of all appearances of conventional reality. In the absence of all conventional appearances, that emptiness can be called "the clear light of the fourth occasion." The Buddhist scholar Sangye Yeshe states that this mind of clear light pervades all of space. This indicates the essential nature, or the mode of being, of the awareness.

One method for arousing such awareness is to recite very sharply the syllable *PHAT*. By doing so, it is said that thoughts are momentarily suspended, and some appearance of emptiness may arise. On such an occasion, even if awareness itself does not manifestly arise, a facsimile of it may. Although at the beginning this is only a facsimile of awareness, by continuing in the practice and becoming more familiar with it, awareness itself will eventually manifest.

The cultivation of meditative concentration is not something separate from the cultivation of mindfulness. The cultivation of mindfulness occurs by not forgetting one's meditative object after one has found it. In his treatise *An Analysis of the Center and the Extremes* (*Madhyānta-vibhaṅga-kārikā*) Maitreya discusses five faults and eight remedies for them in the cultivation of meditative concentration. This shows one very clearly how to cultivate mindfulness. I have discussed these in *Calming the Mind*.

While the main force of one's attention is focused on one's meditative object, another mental factor besides mindfulness is indispensable. One small fraction of the awareness should be directed to the meditating mind itself, to see whether it is becoming excited or lax. This mental factor is called introspection. If one finds that one's attention has drifted away, then it is the function of the introspection to detect this, enabling one to bring it back.

In the cultivation of meditative concentration, two qualities must be cultivated. One of them is attentional stability, which is of a non-conceptual, or non-discursive nature. The second is attentional vividness. These two need to be cultivated and integrated. If one fails to do so, then whatever kind of concentration one cultivates without these, it will not lead to higher and higher realizations.

What is the sign of having gained some progress in the cultivation of non-discursive, non-conceptual, attentional stability? When it seems as if one's awareness merges into the object of one's meditation. To draw an analogy: When one is listening to some extremely beautiful music and is enchanted by this music, it is as if one's awareness dissolves into the music. At that point, one's other sensory faculties, such as vision, are hardly operating. In meditation, if one finds that one's mind seems to become absorbed into the object, this indicates a relatively high degree of attentional stability.

There are two major obstacles for the attainment of such stability. One is called agitation, and the other is excitation. Agitation is any kind of scattering of the attention, which could be due to a wholesome object or an unwholesome object. Excitation entails more specially a kind of attraction to some desirable object. By overcoming these two obstacles of agitation and excitation, attentional stability can be achieved.

As for attentional vividness, this does not refer to the vividness of the appearance of the object, but to the vividness with which the object is apprehended. To draw an analogy: If very strong desire or hostility arises, regardless of how vividly the object appears, the mind is vividly attentive and is strongly committed to its object. Attentional vividness refers to this kind of attentiveness.

There are two hindrances to the cultivation of attentional vividness, both of which make the mind and body heavy and dysfunctional to some extent. Those two qualities are mental dullness and laxity. Dullness is like a gloom, or darkness, that descends upon the mind, whereas laxity is a kind of attentional "fading," in which the full power of vividness is lost. According to the *sūtras*, if one is not able to fully eradicate these two, it is not possible to achieve genuine quiescence.

In Dzogchen practice, the emphasis is on not grasping onto and following after any thoughts concerning the past, and not identifying with thoughts in anticipation of the future. Regarding thoughts concerning the present, whatever conceptualization arises, do not grasp onto it; do not cling to it. If you owned an empty house, you would not have to worry about thieves getting in. Likewise, if you refuse to identify, or to hold on to any conceptualization, your mind becomes like an empty house. The point is simply to maintain this continuity of mindfulness of awareness. To draw an analogy: Space itself is free of grasping and clinging: clouds may arise and clouds may vanish, but the sky does not grasp onto them. Similarly, insofar as the stream of awareness is concerned, if there is no grasping onto conceptualization, thoughts may arise and thoughts may pass, but they do not enter into the nature of the mind.

Since laxity and dullness do not arise in the form of thoughts, the above technique alone may not be effective for dispelling them, so it is important to apply methods that bring forth attentional vividness. It is said that if one cultivates mindfulness alone, attentional vividness will not arise. At times the mind may become depressed and withdraw inwards as a result of laxity, at which point vividness is absent. On such occasions it is good to elate the mind by reflecting upon the benefits of such practice, upon the great opportunity of having a fully endowed human life, and upon the benefits of cultivating a spirit of awakening. By elating the mind, attentional vividness is aroused. One can also counteract laxity simply by taking very good care of one's health, for example by avoiding greasy food, by wearing light clothing, and by meditating in a bright space. This is the way to practice meditation.

Milarepa was a great Tibetan master of Mahāmudrā, which is similar to Dzogchen. On one occasion a disciple of his commented that he took delight in meditating on the *dharmakāya*, or enlightened awareness, but he took no delight in meditating on thoughts, just as he took delight in meditating on the ocean, but not on the waves. This meant that he enjoyed focusing on awareness, but he became disturbed by fluctuations of the conceptual mind. Milarepa encouraged him to regard discursive thoughts as emanations, or expressions, of the *dharmakāya*. The expressions of *dharmakāya* are of the same nature as *dharmakāya*, just as waves are of the same nature as the ocean.

All the four great orders of Tibetan Buddhism, namely, Nyingma, Sakya, Kagyü, and Gelug lead to the same ultimate realization, even though they use somewhat different terminology. Nyingmapas emphasize awareness, Sakyapas emphasize the view of the indivisibility of *saṃsāra* and *nirvāṇa*, Kagyüpas emphasize Mahāmudrā, and Gelugpas emphasize the primordial clear light. All these concepts point to the same ultimate reality.

I would like to dedicate the merit from this presentation to the alleviation of suffering of all beings who are without a protector.

Appendix II
Madhyamaka and Dzogchen

For any type of activity we first need to cultivate the intention to engage in that activity. For mundane activities, generally speaking, one simply intends to get the job done, without concern as to whether one's motivation is wholesome or unwholesome. But for spiritual practice, in which we are concerned with not just short-term results, but with accomplishing an enduring state of well-being, even from lifetime to lifetime, and with eradicating suffering from its very source, the mind is crucial. Thus, for such practice, cultivating a wholesome motivation is very important. Moreover, the Buddha declared that the result of an altruistic motivation is happiness, whereas the result of a negative motivation is unhappiness.

It is said that if one renders service to others, the result is that one receives benefit oneself. On the other hand, if one inflicts harm upon others, that too will return to oneself in the same fashion. Likewise, if one enters into an activity with a disturbed mind, this creates dissatisfaction; one's longing is not fulfilled, and this will eventually lead to regret. On the other hand, if one engages in actions with an altruistic or wholesome motivation, that will eventually give rise to satisfaction. So it is said that the root of Buddha's teachings is compassion.

In fact, the basis of the Śrāvakayāna teachings of Buddhism is avoiding inflicting harm upon others, and in the Mahāyāna teachings, compassion is at the root of all prosperity. This prosperity refers to rebirth in fortunate realms as well as to attaining liberation.

The word "prosperity"(Tib. *bde legs*) is a technical term in Buddhism. Its principle meaning is *nirvāṇa*. In a broader sense, it refers to the fact that the root of all well-being is compassion. The distinction between virtue and non-virtue is not something that one simply knows intuitively; it has to be learned. The ultimate root of happiness and suffering is, respectively, virtue and non-virtue, and to understand the distinction between virtue and non-virtue, one needs a teacher. However, the real distinction between virtue and non-virtue cannot be taught by just anyone; it has to be taught by someone who has reached the highest state of realization. That is, unless the teacher is no longer subject to ignorance, it is very difficult for one to infallibly distinguish between virtue and non-virtue. The only kind of person who is utterly free of confusion is a spiritually awakened being, a *buddha*. The root of attaining spiritual awakening is compassion, and once one has attained that state one shows others the way to liberation in accordance with their specific, individual capacities, predilections, and interests. By doing so, one shows them the ways of virtue and non-virtue, and shows them how to abandon one and cultivate the other, which thereby brings them happiness and alleviates their suffering. So, in that sense it is said that the root of all well-being is compassion.

Under the influence of great compassion, if one is motivated to cultivate the wholesome and abandon the unwholesome for the sake of other sentient beings, then by means of such practice one is able to eradicate what are called the cognitive obscurations (Tib. *shes bya'i sgrib pa*). In this way, one can attain full awakening and realize one's full capacity for being of service to others. Moreover, compassion protects one from the extreme of quietism. The extreme of quietism is *nirvāṇa*. The fact that the wisdom that realizes emptiness does on occasion lead to the attainment of buddhahood is because of its companion, namely great compassion. It is also true that great compassion leads to the attainment of perfect awakening of a *buddha* because of its companion, the wisdom that realizes emptiness. Cultivating the two, both skillful means and wisdom, brings about both near-term, temporal benefits, as well as long-term, ultimate benefits. Therefore, one's spiritual path must at all times entail a union of skillful means and wisdom. These two are indispensable for bringing the path to its culmination. As much as one is drawn to the realization of emptiness, so should one complement that with an emphasis on the cultivation of compassion.

We can see in the world that compassion is something of great importance, that it provides a real source of refuge or protection for sentient beings. Doesn't it seem true that if we show kindness and compassion to others, this leads others to well-being and alleviates their suffering? Likewise, if others show us kindness, that leads to the alleviation of our own suffering and to our own well-being. So if we are really concerned with the well-being of humanity and of the whole world, then the cultivation of compassion is really important. Please cultivate such a motivation of compassion, a motivation of altruism, even for receiving these teachings.

I would now like to discuss the Madhyamaka view. For one who has taken the *bodhisattva* precepts there is a restriction concerning speaking about the view of emptiness. Nevertheless, I trust that those who read this are capable of critical inquiry, in which case I feel I can speak freely. So that I do not break this *bodhisattva* vow, I ask you to avoid the conclusion that this view is promoting a nihilistic view of total non-existence. Moreover, please abandon the notion that since all phenomena are empty, there are no consequences of well-being from virtuous deeds and no consequences of suffering from nonvirtuous deeds. If we can avoid drawing such false conclusions, then we can proceed.

If something can have emptiness as its ultimate nature, it is capable of performing various types of functions. In contrast, if there were something whose ultimate nature was not emptiness, it would be incapable of performing any function. So we should recognize that the fact that phenomena have emptiness as their ultimate nature is the very quality that makes their interaction possible; it is in fact necessary for them to be able to enter into action and perform any variety of functions.

I would now like to offer a critical comparison between two Buddhist systems, Dzogchen, or the Great Perfection, and Madhyamaka, or the Middle Way. Through such a comparison, we can see to what extent these two views have a common basis.

The basis upon which these teachings will be offered is the notion of the Two Truths. A *sūtra* states, "The phenomena revealed by the Buddha are included within the division of the Two Truths." This means that all phenomena of *saṃsāra* and of *nirvāṇa* are included in these Two Truths. And what are these Two Truths? They are ultimate truth and conventional truth. Ultimate truth refers to an object of the mind that is authentic and without deception. In terms of the objects of the mind, ultimate truth refers to emptiness. In fact, according to the Prāsaṅgika Madhyamaka view, apart from the mind that perceptually realizes emptiness, there is no cognition among sentient beings that is free from deception. Thus, all other phenomena, such as those that are objects of the six senses, are included in what is called conventional truth.

In terms of the bases of emptiness, one can speak of the self and other phenomena. Correspondingly, one can speak of personal identitylessness and phenomenal identitylessness. In this regard the "I" is a conventional truth, and the absence, or emptiness, of an inherent "I" is ultimate truth. But now we need something upon which we designate the "I," called the basis of designation of the "I," and that is not the "I" itself, but rather the psycho-physical aggregates; the lack of inherent existence of those aggregates is called phenomenal identitylessness. The identitylessness of the "I" described above is thus personal identitylessness, while the identityless-ness of the aggregates is phenomenal identitylessness. More-over, the bases of designation of the "I," namely the aggregates, or more simply, the body and mind, fall into the category of conventional truth. The distinction between the two types of identitylessness, personal identitylessness and phenomenal identitylessness, is made not with regard to what is not present or absent, but with regard to the basis of emptiness. In other words, it is not a different type of emptiness; it is simply a different basis that has emptiness as its ultimate nature.

All phenomena are included within the Two Truths. This includes, for example, the attainment of perfect spiritual awak-ening and the path of awakening. By failing to ascertain the nature of the Two Truths, one continues to cycle in *saṃsāra*. But by overcoming one's confusion concerning the Two Truths, one perfects the two principle aspects of the path, namely skill-ful means and wisdom.

How does confusion arise concerning the Two Truths? We can ask this question in relation to the "I." How does the "I" exist? First of all, the "I" does not exist except as a conceptual or verbal designation. Apart from that, the "I" has no other mode of existence. However, by falsely grasping onto the "I" as being truly existent, then other mental afflictions arise, such as attachment and anger. Verbal and physical actions are aroused by such afflictive mind states. These in turn leave habitual propensities upon the mind, and these habitual pro-pensities are catalyzed by conditions, which leads to future rebirth. In this way, the cycle of *saṃsāra* is perpetuated.

To draw a classic analogy for that false mode of apprehen-sion of the "I," one may see a coiled striped rope as a snake, and because one apprehends it as a snake, the emotional re-sponses of fear and anger and the wish to kill it arise. How-ever, if one recognized the striped rope as a rope from the outset, and recognized from the beginning that there was no snake, then no fear would arise, and similarly, no anger and no wish to kill would arise either. To give another example, if one is in darkness and sees some yellowish object, one might falsely apprehend it as gold, so craving for it may arise. But again, if one could see clearly, one would recognize that there is no gold, and the ensuing desire would not arise. In both of these cases, the appearance belies the reality; there is in fact no snake, and similarly the yellowish substance, although it has the appearance of gold, is not in fact gold. In each case, if one recognized the deceptive nature of appearances from the outset, the anger or desire would not arise.

Thus, in the absence of confusion, neither attachment nor hostility arise, which means that no verbal or physical activity stemming from those mental afflictions would arise either. However, if the mental affliction of attachment or anger does arise, suffering is produced. If one can recognize that the reality of suffering arises from *karma*, and that *karma* arises from mental afflictions, then one can recognize how these mental afflictions arise. This gives rise to a wish to be free of the sources of one's suffering.

If we look at the aspects of skillful means and wisdom of the Śrāvaka and Pratyekabuddha paths, their skillful means consists of their ardent yearning to be free of the cycle of existence and to attain *nirvāṇa*, and that motivation is called a spirit of emergence. For totally eradicating suffering from its roots, one must have the motivation of a spirit of emergence. The *bodhisattva*'s spirit of awakening is not indispensable for cutting the root of suffering. There are two aspects for pursuing any kind of activity: getting rid of unfavorable conditions, and cultivating favorable conditions. For the task of attaining spiritual awakening, the function of realizing emptiness is to eradicate the principle unfavorable circumstances; the function of a spirit of emergence and a spirit of awakening is to bring about favorable circumstances. So for both Hīnayāna and Mahāyāna practitioners, the realization of emptiness is not sufficient for achieving their respective goals. Moreover, it is possible to realize emptiness even if one is not a Buddhist.

By reflecting upon the manner in which other sentient beings are brought into suffering and by seeing that they are dominated by mental afflictions such as attachment and anger, compassion arises. Attending to the suffering of others and not being able to bear their suffering and afflictions is the mental state called compassion. From compassion for others naturally arises the wish to bring others happiness and to relieve their suffering.

But then, when one reviews one's own abilities, one sees that one is not in a position to be effective in relieving the suffering of others; when one then reflects about who has such an ability, one recognizes that a *buddha*, a fully enlightened being, has that ability. As a result the aspiration for spiritual awakening arises since that is the way to be of greatest possible service to other beings. This is the type of motivation that arises on the Mahāyāna path of a *bodhisattva*.

Returning to the example of the "I," the "I" exists only as a conceptual or verbal designation. It has no true existence apart from that. Let's set up a hypothetical situation in which the "I" does not merely exist as a conceptual or verbal designation, but truly exists. What would it be like? What would follow? If the "I" truly existed, then we would have what is called a "word of truth" (Tib. *bden tshig*). What does this imply? A word of truth creates a truth. And what does this imply? It implies that is an exact corroboration between what one is seeing and the reality that it represents. Moreover, this would be an immutable truth.

Ignorance apprehends phenomena as being truly existent, as intrinsically or inherently existent, as existing by their own characteristics. When we apprehend the "I" as being truly existent, it appears as something that is simply there on its own. If there were an "I" that existed in a fashion corresponding to the way that it is apprehended by ignorance, it would have to be immutable. Holding that type of changeless "I" in mind, with what can we equate the "I"? Can we equate it with the body, or can we equate it with the mind? As soon as we enter into such an analysis, there is no such "I" to be found. As we seek out how such an "I" might exist, or where it might exist, we find that it is not to be equated with the body, nor with the collection of body and mind. However, if we look for such an "I" totally separate from the body and mind, we find that it cannot be established there either. So the "I" that is grasped by ignorance turns out to be nowhere to be found.

When you say "my collection of body and mind," aren't you already implying that the "I" who has them is separate from the actual collection of body and mind that you have? It is a matter of phrasing. You say on the one hand "I," and then on the other hand you say, "the body and mind which I have." They seem to be distinct. And that is true of anything else, whenever you speak of parts and the whole. The whole of the entity is that which has all the parts. This is easier to recognize in reference to a person, because one can more easily discern the distinction between "I" and "mine." But it is equally applicable for other things.

Take a pen as an example. You can say that the pen is a collection of all its parts, but we still regard the pen as that which *has* the collection of its parts. If you identify the "I" as the collection of body and mind, what really is the nature of the collection that you are identifying? Is it a collection simply of all the parts of the body? Or is it a collection of all the parts of the mind? And is that collection of all the components of the body and mind itself something that is truly existent? If the collection of body and mind is itself truly existent, this would imply that if you isolate the *collection* of body and mind from the body and from the mind, there would be something left over, namely the collection of the two. Thus, the collection itself is merely a designation, and it is not identical with either the body or the mind. It cannot be equated with either, yet it exists in dependence upon them and it does not exist apart from them.

It is said that such a deceptive phenomenon that is merely designated is nevertheless able to perform all of its functions. Before we have the label of a pen, for example, there is no way to talk about a pen writing, or a pen having ink, or anything else. But as soon as we have designated that label "pen," we can talk about everything a pen does: it writes, it has ink, and so forth. Relating this to the individual, if a specific individual does not have a name, we still have the general name "human being," so we can speak of the human being going, the human being doing this, doing that, and so forth. But as soon as that individual has been named—let's say, has been given the name Tashi—only from that point on can we say, "Tashi is going," "Tashi is sitting," "Tashi is eating," and so forth. As soon as we have agreed upon the convention that this person is named Tashi, we can agree upon the other conventions of sitting, drinking, and so forth. All of these come about merely by the force of convention, or social agreement. Without such a convention, or agreement, it is impossible to identify anything. Thus, since I am Tibetan, if you don't speak Tibetan, we have nothing to say at all, and the reason for that is that we don't have a conventional agreement on what anything means. We cannot identify anything. What is missing here is a conventional agreement about the relationship between a name and a designated object. But there still arises a sense—whether or not we have made such a conventional agreement of applying labels to objects—that there seems to be something really out there. But even that basic sense of something being there relies upon the convention of something really being there. In contrast, if one has no conventions at all, then all functions, all activities, simply vanish.

When the ignorance that falsely apprehends the "I" as truly existent is active, the mental afflictions of attachment and anger arise. So during many lifetimes, from the past to the present, our minds and our ignorance have been close companions. Nevertheless, ignorance is not of the very nature of the mind. It is not true that this ignorance cannot be separated from the mind, or from the stream of consciousness.

According to the Prāsaṅgika Madhyamaka system, by realizing the nonexistence of the object that is apprehended by ignorance, a realization arises that is called the Madhyamaka View, or the view of the Middle Way. And the object of this subjective view, which is the nonexistence of the object grasped by ignorance, is emptiness. In terms of that emptiness, there is no distinction between the Madhyamaka view and the Dzogchen view.

According to the great Gelugpa scholar Khedrup Je, emptiness is like the center of space which cannot be recognized, meaning that if one analyzes the nature of reality, there is nothing to be recognized. The implication is that if one does not engage in such an analysis, then phenomena can be established as existent, but if one analyzes phenomena, they cannot be established or recognized as existent.

If one takes as an example a pen, here is something that has been designated, and you can say, "This is a pen." If you do not probe into the nature of it, then the pen can easily be established as existent. In that sense it exists. If one simply tries to establish whether or not this is a pen, this is still on the conventional level. But once you have designated something as a pen, if you are not satisfied with that, you may start to probe more deeply and ask, "Which part is a pen? Is it the upper part or the lower part? The inside or the outside?" Then the pen is not to be found. This is also what the great Nyingmapa scholar Longchen Rabjampa meant when he said, "When you investigate, there is nothing to recognize."

The Prāsaṅgika Madhyamaka system says perhaps more clearly that phenomena do exist for the mind that does not analyze phenomena in that latter fashion. Therefore, one should be satisfied with the mere verbal imputation. That is, once you have designated something as an object without engaging in the latter type of analysis, one should be satisfied; then the object that one has so designated is able to perform the functions that one attributes to it. However, when one is not satisfied with allowing the pen to do the job of a pen, and asks, "What is the pen?" there is nothing that can be identified as a pen.

Once again, in terms of establishing the nature of emptiness, there is no distinction between the Dzogchen view and the Madhyamaka view. The nineteenth-century Tibetan Dzogchen master Dodrubchen investigated the philosophy of Longchen Rabjampa and his spiritual lineage, and declared that emptiness can be chiefly understood as a simple negation, a sheer absence of true existence.

Longchen Rabjampa and his school philosophically present emptiness chiefly as a simple negation, but for the actual meditation on emptiness, he treats it chiefly as a complex negation. Let's review these two terms, which are not self-explanatory. What is meant by saying that emptiness is to be established as a simple negation? It means that as one analytically probes the nature of the inherently existent self, one finds that it does not exist as the body, or as the mind, or as the combination of the two, or as anything else. From this type of analysis one comes to the conclusion that the inherently existent self does not exist. The mere absence of such an "I" is the simple negation of such an inherently existent "I." That is emptiness.

By meditating on emptiness the mere absence of an inherently existent "I" appears to the mind. One does not identify the absence of such inherent existence and then add to that some idea of emptiness, or a notion that the aggregates do exist. If one did so, that would be a complex negation, whereas emptiness is a simple negation.

The Madhyamaka system says that emptiness should be regarded as a simple negation, not only for theoretically establishing the nature of emptiness, but also for meditating on emptiness. However, in contrast, according to the Dzogchen system, as one meditates on emptiness, one regards it chiefly as a complex negation. Now, if one establishes emptiness as a complex negation, this means that one is negating something, namely inherent existence, and one is affirming something else. So it is complex in the sense that you are negating one thing, while affirming another. It is said that the awareness with which one meditates on emptiness in Dzogchen practice is far more subtle than the awareness with which one meditates on emptiness according to the Madhyamaka view practiced in the Sūtrayāna.

Let's look at Dzogchen meditation on the nature of the mind, in which one examines three topics:

• The source from which the mental events arise.
• The domain in which mental events are present.
• That into which mental events disappear.

If you can establish the basis from which the mental events arise, then you can say that it is truly existent. Or, if you can establish the domain in which mental events exist right now, you can say that this is truly existent. Or, if you can establish a reality into which mental events disappear, you can establish the mind as being truly existent. Seeking these bases, corresponding to the past, present, and future of mental events, and not finding them is itself the very process of meditation. In this way one recognizes the unfindability of the true existence of the mind. In this practice one makes a distinction between what is simply called mind (Tib. *sems*), and the ground into which the mind, or all mental events, vanishes. That ground is called awareness (Tib. *rig pa*). It is not so much that the mind is unfindable under analysis; it is more as if it simply vanishes into space. Once one has identified that ground into which the mind vanishes as awareness, how is emptiness established? When awareness is identified and manifests, all appearances and concepts of conventional reality vanish.

According to the New Translation School of Tibetan Buddhism, in order for the innate mind to manifest, it is necessary to bring an end to all conceptualization. Following the complete cessation of thoughts, a most subtle degree of awareness called clear light manifests. It is also called the innate mind. According to Dodrubchen, the innate mind discussed in such tantric systems as Cakrasaṃvara and Guhyasamāja is identical with the awareness discussed in the Dzogchen system. Some people say that when conceptualization vanishes and the innate mind manifests, there is an appearance of emptiness.

The innate mind manifests even for non-meditators, or ordinary human beings, at the time of death. At that time, when the innate mind manifests, some people say that emptiness appears to that mind, but this seems debatable. However, whether or not emptiness appears when the innate mind manifests, one is not able to distinguish one thing from another, for the conceptual mind is dormant. That state of awareness is somewhat akin to the state of mind in deep sleep, in that all conceptual processes have vanished and one experiences something resembling a nonconceptual realization of emptiness. The term "conceptualization" is designated upon a variety of mental processes. All mental afflictions are called conceptualization, and in the context of the Dzogchen teachings, even meditative quiescence focused on emptiness itself would be called conceptualization. Although the cultivation of meditative quiescence subdues thoughts, the Dzogchen tradition says this simply means that conceptual, analytical processes have been subdued. In the practice of quiescence, when you have the sense of the meditating mind dissolving into the object, this is sometimes said to be nonconceptual, because thoughts no longer arise, but the Dzogchen masters say that conceptualization is still present.

In Vajrayāna practice, according to the New Translation School, there is a phase in which one imagines emitting rays of light from one's heart throughout the universe, then draws them in and dissolves them into one's heart. Sequentially, one dissolves all of these appearances into the innate mind, and imagines dissolving them into a *nāda* [the curved line above such Tibetan and Sanskrit syllables as *hūṃ*], which finally vanishes into emptiness, in which all conceptualization ceases.

Tsongkhapa says of a meditator who realizes emptiness that such a *yogin* must have first gained a profound understanding of the manner in which those empty phenomena exist as dependently related events. Furthermore, one must have realized that those phenomena which are dependently related events are by nature empty of inherent existence. A person who has realized this and enters into the tantric practice of dissolving all appearances into the *nāda* and dissolving that into emptiness, actually realizes emptiness at that point.

According to the Dzogchen tradition, this disappearance into emptiness is the innate mind. This tradition makes a distinction between mind (Tib. *sems*) and awareness (Tib. *rig pa*). The former refers to the dualistic, conceptual mind, while awareness refers to the ground of the appearances to the mind and the ground into which the conceptual mind vanishes.

According to Dodrubchen, when awareness manifests, one does not apprehend the absence of a truly existent subject and object. However, since one has identified the ground of the mind, awareness, the wisdom that realizes emptiness rises up like a flame. That, in short, is how one can unify the Dzogchen and the Madhyamaka approaches.

Any contemplative who has identified awareness has necessarily realized emptiness. However, any person who has gained a realization of emptiness by means of the Sūtrayāna approach has not necessarily identified awareness. To evaluate these two approaches in terms of their capacity to dispel the obscurations of the mind, the awareness that manifests in Dzogchen practice, which is unmoved by conceptualization, is far more potent for dispelling the obscurations of the mind, and in that sense it is regarded as far more profound. In comparison to that, the type of awareness cultivated through the Sūtrayāna methods is not as subtle as that of the Dzogchen methods, and therefore it is not as effective in terms of dispelling the obscurations of the mind.

Nevertheless, there is no distinction between these two approaches in terms of the view of emptiness. Moreover, the essential purpose of both types of meditation is to cut ignorance at its root. However, there is a distinction in terms of the meditating mind and the process of meditation. If your practice is not getting at the root of ignorance, then it does not matter whether you are practicing Dzogchen or Madhyamaka. And for these two systems there is very little distinction between their ways of presenting conventional reality. They both state that phenomena exist by the power of conceptual and verbal designations. Also, both state that in dependence upon the accumulation of knowledge the *jñānadharmakāya* arises as a *buddha,* and in dependence upon the collection of merit the *rūpakāya* arises. Both of these assertions stem from a common understanding of the Two Truths. Based upon these one can speak of the two aspects of the path, namely skillful means and wisdom, and one can speak of the two aspects of the fruition, namely the body and the mind of a *buddha.*